Invasion of the Head-Scratchers

Invasion of the Head-Scratchers: Survivors' Guide to Scholarship Essays

Copyright © 2015 by Unique Ink Publishing. All rights reserved.
ISBN 13-978-1-939957-01-6

Unique Ink Publishing
Roosevelt High School
6941 N. Central St. Portland, OR 97203
(503) 916-5260
www.rooseveltroughwriters.org/unique-ink-publishing

Lead Editors: Sedge Carver, Carlee Durkee, Gameti Kalil and Jocelyn Loyd

Contributing Authors:
Andriana Alexis
Devashna Anand
Sedge Carver
Carlee Durkee
Aojah Hill
Gameti Kalil
Izabella Larsen
Jocelyn Loyd
Espoir David Mbirize
Mariah Radkey
Kyrah Saito
Anthony Sylvester
Morgan Yamamoto

Cover Illustration: Brian Parker
Design: Pamela Pfiffner, Bespoke Books Publishing Co.
Photography: Kate McPherson
Visual Concepts: Aojah Hill, Brian Parker and Lorelei White
Illustrations: Brian Parker

For information regarding special purchases of *Invasion of the Head-Scratchers*, contact Unique Ink at the address above.

All proceeds from the sale of this book support Roosevelt High School's Writing and Publishing Center.

Printed in the United States of America.

Invasion of the Head-Scratchers

Survivors' Guide to Scholarship Essays

SCHOLARSHIP AWARDS

Angel Bibiano-Marcial - Dr. Ethel Simon McWilliams S...
Isaiah Eddington - Beat the Odds Scholarship
Christie Jackson - Asuza Pacific Univ Director's Scho...
                   Concordia Deans Merit Scholars...
Abigail Pasion -   Comcast Leader & Achiever Schola...
                   Dr. John Garlington Diversity Award
                   Lee Leadership Scholarship
                   Drama Scholarship Award
                   ACT Six
                   Warner Pacific Merit Awa...

Sione Taumoe'anga - PSU Scholarship
Semise Kofe   - PSU Scholarship
Lucia Fonon   - UP Presidential Sch...
                   Warner/George Fox Scholarship
Melissa DeLara-Vargas - Bruin Scholarship
                   Chaminade Scholarship

Etsegenet Ayele - PLU Scholarship   Dell Scholarship   RHS Womens Scho...

Melisa Hna   - Pacific University Scholarship   Asian Reporter Scholarship

Brandon Saephan - PSU Diversity Scholarship

Leroy Brandon   - OSU Diversity Scholarship   GATES Scholarship

Ashley Van Horn - Al Forthan Memorial Scholarship - Kaiser Scholarship

Daryl Maplethorpe   OSAC   Nathan Buckland - Mock Scholars...

> Did you know that students in the 2014 class of Roosevelt High School earned more than *$5 million* in scholarships? And did you know that the RHS class of 2015 received more than *$6 million* in scholarships?
>
> **Six million dollars!**

Contents

This Book is a Resource	**7**
Naviance: A Very Important Resource	7
Letter to the Reader	**9**
High School Timeline	**11**
Scholarship Qualifications	**13**
Tackling the Scholarship	**15**
No Scholarship? Get a Grant	16
What About Student Loans?	17
Successful Scholarship Essays	**19**
Portland State University Diversity Scholarship	19
Future Connect Scholarship	20
Peninsula Optimist Club Scholarship	21
César E. Chávez Leadership Conference Scholarship	23
Kaiser Permanente Health Care Career Scholarship	24
Beat the Odds Scholarship	25
Gates Millennium Scholarship	27
QuestBridge National College Match	30
Bank of America Joe Martin Scholarship	31
Theodore Roosevelt Women's Scholarship	33
OSAC (Office of Student Access and Completion) Scholarships	35
Words of Wisdom	**40**
Words of Wisdom from Past Seniors	40
Words of Wisdom from Teachers	40
Personal Statements	**43**
Student Examples	45
Scholarship Information	**46**
State and Local Scholarships	46
Act Six Portland	46
Al Forthan Memorial Scholarship	46
Beat the Odds Scholarship	47
Black United Fund Scholarships	47
Ron Herndon Scholarship	47
ACCESS Scholarships	48
Inspiring Hope Scholarship	48
César E. Chávez Leadership Conference Scholarship (CECLC)	49
Dr. Ethel Simon-McWilliams Scholarship	49
Education First Scholarship	49
Future Connect Scholarship	50
Hispanic Metropolitan Chamber Scholarship	50
Kaiser Permanente Health Care Career Scholarship	50

Contents

State and Local Scholarships, continued
- Neil Kelly Memorial Scholarship (Albina Rotary Scholarship) — 51
- OSAC (Office of Student Access and Completion) — 51
- Skanner Foundation Scholarship — 53

National Scholarships — 53
- Dell Scholars Program — 53
- Gates Millennium Scholarship — 53
- National Health Corps Scholarships — 54
- QuestBridge National College Match — 54

College-Specific Scholarships — 55
- Academic Scholarships — 55
- Portland Community College — 55
- Mt. Hood Community College — 57
- Clackamas Community College — 57

Other Scholarship Opportunities — 58
- Diversity Scholarships — 58
- Immigration Status Scholarships — 58
- Employee-Dependent Scholarships — 58
- Optimist Scholarship — 59
- Roosevelt-Specific Scholarships — 59

Letters of Recommendation — 61
- Tips for Getting Good Letters — 61
- Sample Letters of Recommendation — 61

So, That's It? — 64
Glossary — 66
Thanks — 67
About Us — 68
- Roosevelt High School's Writing and Publishing Center — 68
- Roosevelt High School's Summer Internship — 69

This Book is a Resource

Invasion of the Head-Scratchers serves as a powerful resource and is designed for students who are writing college scholarship essays. Featuring winning essays written by Roosevelt High School graduates, this book will help you brainstorm and find inspiration for your writing.

A team of Roosevelt students, mentored by students of Portland State University's Ooligan Press, pieced together **winning scholarship essays into a resource for people who are applying for scholarships**. This book aims to help different kinds of students, from those with a 4.0 GPA to a 1.0 GPA, and is a reminder that college is attainable regardless of background, grades or income. It also provides inspiration for writing your own essays.

Writing a scholarship essay does not come with instructions. The essay prompt will tell you what to include, and your teachers will tell you what to brag about, but the words have to come from you. Scholarship essays are used for the sole purpose of seeing if you are the right person to receive the award. **This means you have to show, not tell.** Showing the obstacles you've faced, ways you've helped the community and the leadership qualities you have is better than telling about them. Your experiences have to come to life through words. A lot of the time, the words are hard to find.

We wrote this book to help students find the right words and to make sure their essays are worthy of cash prizes. Whether you're trying to maneuver through the scholarship application process or just to get your foot in the door, use this book as a guide on how to write essays, and as a resource for finding the scholarships that are right for you. While writing countless essays may seem like a bore and a waste of time, words can pave the way to college and open the door to interesting and creative jobs. The essays in this book are the actual words that several RHS students used to pave their way to college.

Naviance: A Very Important Resource

To start the scholarship process, you need to get familiar with Naviance. **Naviance is a free college- and career-readiness resource that many high schools, including Roosevelt, use to help with high school, college and professional success.** To use this online resource, you have to register through your school counselor for an account and password. It is a tool that should be used throughout all four years of high school. Not only is Naviance useful for creating a resume and researching colleges and scholarships, but it also stores your information so that when you apply, you will have the work ready to use. It can also be used to request transcripts and letters of recommendation for scholarships and colleges.

Naviance tends to be a tool used primarily for seniors, but **the goal is that all RHS students will use it all four years of high school**. Seniors use this source to complete many graduation requirements like exit surveys, resumes and Career Related Learning Experience Reflections. Seniors can also request their transcripts for college applications and scholarships through the Naviance tool. At Roosevelt, school counselors also use it to send out information about local and national scholarship opportunities, as well as internships, college visits, job opportunities and much more!

Not knowing how this student resource works by your junior and senior year can make it quite difficult to use it to your benefit. Some of the challenges both students and parents run into when using Naviance include forgetting a password or not knowing how to navigate the site. In order to prevent these issues, **school counselors suggest you log in two to three times per week and become familiar with how Naviance works.**

> "I used Naviance at least three times a week to see if I had fulfilled all my graduation requirements and to see if there are any scholarships available that I qualified for."

Note to Readers: If you do not attend a Portland Public School or your school does not have Naviance, ask your school counselor to find out if your school has another web-based system for tracking scholarship information.

"Money doesn't have to be an issue when it comes to pursuing higher education. Now I have enough scholarships and grants to pay all my expenses for my first year at an awesome university."

"Some students shy away from scholarships because they doubt their accomplishments. They hear about the thespian/volunteer/athlete/student body president/valedictorian who won the big bucks. Never quit before you even start. Many students demonstrate their best qualities in very ordinary activities."

"Scholarships are dreadful. I was rejected more than awarded, and sometimes it hurt.. You will want to quit, but it's worth it in the end."

"I think a lot of people who write these essays say they have always known they have wanted to be a doctor or a lawyer, but in reality, a lot of college students are going through the same crisis, unsure of what they wanted to do. Saying he didn't know made the essay more relatable."

"Join lots of clubs/sports/activities, go find volunteer work to do, write down what you did and then start early on writing the scholarship essays so you have time to write and refine them."

"In my scholarship essays, I need to write why I chose to do the career I chose, but first, I need to figure out why I chose it in the first place. Lastly, I need to get comfortable with bragging."

"Attend classes. Do your best. Be involved with a variety of activities. Find your passion. Pursue it without abandon! Then search for every scholarship under the sun and apply, apply, apply! They can't give you money if you don't go after it."

"Work hard to have a good GPA throughout high school, starting with your freshman year. It's easier to get scholarships with a good GPA, and it's harder to make up lost ground later."

"Get those scholarships done as soon as possible. Get down to them at least a month before they're due. If you get it done and you think it's complete, revise it at least three or four times to make it better."

"The scholarship process was challenging, but worth it. My advice to you is don't procrastinate. Be yourself and put your heart into your essays."

"Do your scholarships on time, know the deadlines, get everything for the scholarship, just get it done."

Letter to the Reader

Dear Scholar,

I have good news, but let's start with the bad news.

There is no ultimate secret formula to win over scholarship committees nor is there a single source for all the right words. There is no guarantee that you will cash in every time, even if you think about it to the brink of insanity.

It's rather depressing, even soul crushing, to receive a letter — and sometimes an email — of rejection. That doesn't mean you're a failure and should give up completely on becoming more than a wide-eyed burger flipper. I'm not going to patronize you by promising that everything works out in the end, even if it does.

Now for the good news. You hold in your hands a book that can help you get the funds to go to college so that you won't have to worry about living in your parent's basement all your life.

In this book you will find application tips, advice and examples of scholarship essays that have been accepted. The best part is that they're all original, unedited and are actually written by students — not by English teachers without summer plans.

This resource guide was made for students with the intention of actually being useful. So take the time to review the scholarship prompt before you move on to the essay. Soak it in. Mull it over. Plus, it wouldn't hurt to research the listed scholarships. You never know what you may find. You could run into a dead end, or you might find everything you are looking for, but you'll never know if you don't take the initiative to find out for yourself.

Good luck!

Jocelyn Loyd

*Roosevelt High School
Class of 2013*

"My freshman year was very challenging. I honestly thought I wasn't going to attend college, let alone finish high school. After a few bumps and turns on my 'road to graduation,' I discovered my talents and realized that anything is possible if I work smarter, instead of just harder, for it."

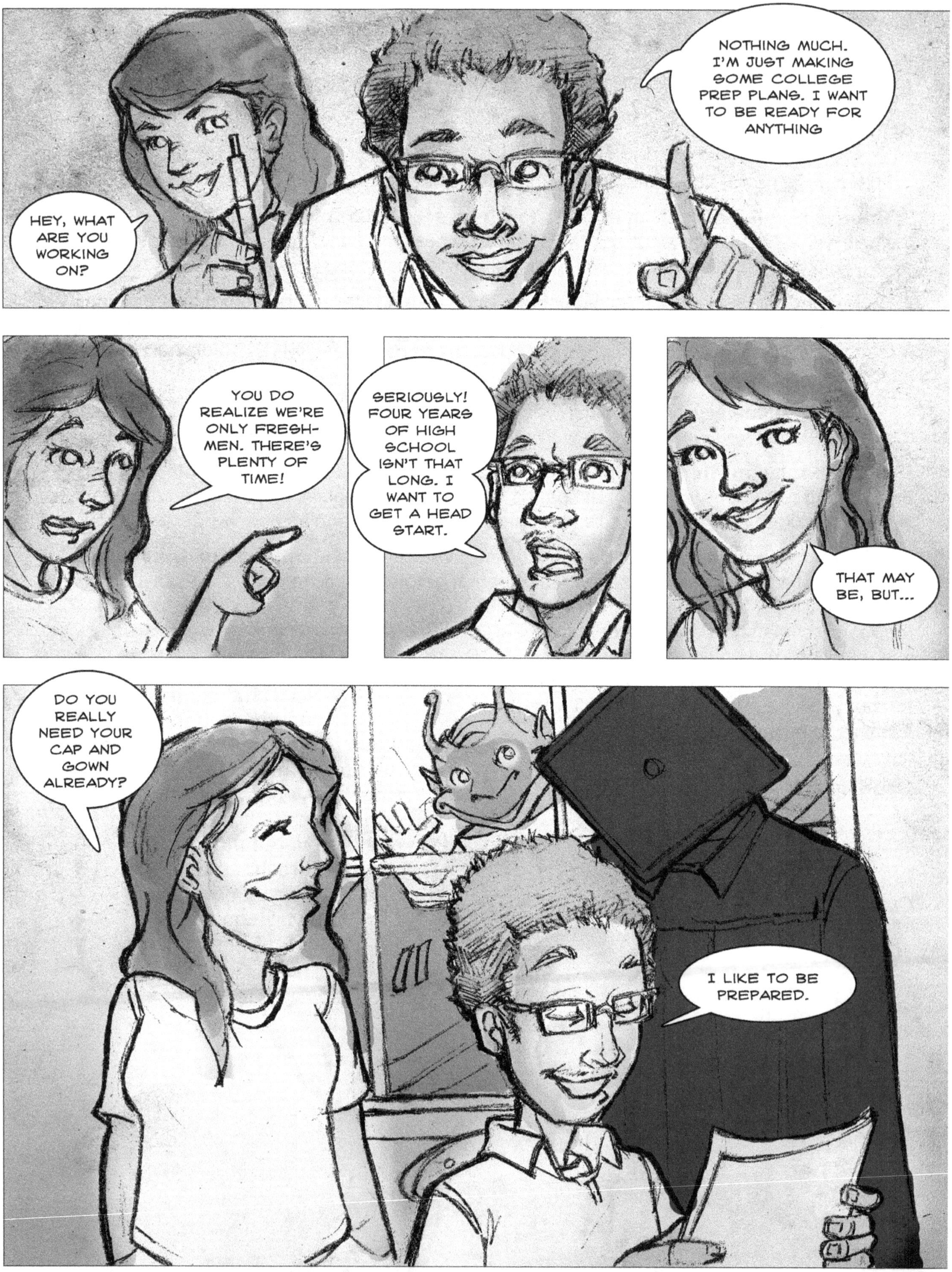

High School Timeline

Notes

Many people, including parents, ask what high school students should be doing to get into college, to apply for strong scholarships and to maintain success in school. The following list indicates the activities high school students should be doing in order to be successful in high school and college.

Important No Matter Your Grade

Stay on top of schoolwork.

No matter if you're freshman or a senior, being responsible when it comes to schoolwork will help you more than almost anything else. Turn your work in on time, study, strive for good grades, stay organized and make sure you've got all the credits you need each year. If you start out on the right foot, you'll avoid a lot of hassle later. It is much harder to raise a low GPA than to earn a solid GPA each year.

Stay healthy: mentally, physically and emotionally.

The fact of the matter is that you're always going to learn better when you're happy, healthy and well-rested. You're much more likely to succeed if you get eight or more hours of sleep, eat a healthy breakfast and stay relaxed and relatively stress-free.

Volunteer!

Your volunteer work can make or break a scholarship application. Colleges are looking for people who are active, interested and driven to help in their community. Being a part of your community, while also teaching you valuable skills for the future, can make your scholarship application shine.

Freshman (9th Grade)

Get familiar with resources that can help you.

Your school has many resources — including your counselor and college-preparation programs like GEAR UP, Step Up, AVID and the Writing Center — to help you be the best student you can possibly be. You can also seek out teachers, coaches, family members and friends who can be your allies through your years in high school. Look into these resources and utilize them. Knowing what you have at your disposal will make things much easier.

Get involved with your community.

Freshman year is a good time to get involved with clubs and other extracurricular activities. In your later high school years, volunteer work will be vital, but as a freshman, the best thing you can do is get comfortable with your school and your community through sports and clubs.

Develop good learning habits.

It might seem trivial now, but if you develop positive learning habits early, you can save yourself a lot of stress later. Know how you learn best and advocate for that sort of environment in your classroom. Find a quiet, comfortable place where you can get homework done after school or find a group of friends who can help you study. Learn about study techniques and note-taking skills that help with test taking. All of this knowledge will be priceless in your future scholastic endeavors.

Begin to think about and prepare for your future in high school, college and beyond.

During freshman year, most of your focus should be on getting comfortable with high school and not preparing for the future. However, it can be helpful to create a resume freshman year that can be updated as you progress through high school. It's also a good idea to research summer opportunities, such as internships, volunteer work and jobs to keep you busy during the break.

Notes

Sophomore (10th Grade)

Continue to use school and community resources.

It's a good idea to get familiar with Naviance and use it on a regular basis. In addition, keep in contact with teachers and school counselors who may be able to help you. As you begin to think more about your future, you should meet with your school counselor to talk about your transcript, credits and your plan for college.

Stay involved in your community.

Now that the craziness of freshman year is over, the time has come to buckle down and start seriously looking at some volunteer opportunities. The earlier you start, the better. You will be thankful later when you have lots of hours of community service under your belt. If you don't know where to start, ask your school counselor or check out Hands On Portland (www.handsonportland.org) or do some research on your own about opportunities in your area. Join a club like Key Club, Honors Society or MEChA because they are actively involved in the community. Be sure to document on your resume both the service you have done and what you learned, and store your resume in Naviance.

Practice the good learning strategies you learned in Freshman year.

Along with knowing how and where you learn best and getting in the habit of doing your work and turning it in on time, it's also helpful to put an emphasis on taking notes and using them to study. You'll do much better on important tests if you study regularly.

Start to prepare for your future in high school and college.

If you didn't create a resume during freshman year, create one now. If you already have a resume, update it with missing information. Think about which colleges sound like viable options for you and investigate ways to pay your tuition through scholarships and financial aid. Also, decide if you want to take any special classes like Advanced Placement classes or dual-credit classes that provide college credit for your course work.

Junior (11th Grade)

Continue to use school and community resources.

As always, it's important to keep a good relationship with your school counselor and teachers. Your teachers can write letters of recommendation and your school counselor can discuss your transcript and your future plan for graduation.

Community involvement is crucial.

You should definitely have some volunteer hours already recorded, and you should start assuming a leadership role in clubs and service activities. Attending events that can help you figure out your college plan, like the Junior Symposium and the Spring College Fair, and visiting universities can give you valuable information about college.

Make sure you have a clear idea of what you want out of the rest of your high school experience and begin to think about college.

The more you plan during junior year, the less hectic senior year will be, so make sure that you've completed your personal statement and Office of Student Access and Completion (OSAC) essays for getting into college, as well your scholarship applications. Update your resume, keep researching financial aid options and do last-minute forecasting for any rigorous courses you might be interested in taking during your senior year.

Senior (12th Grade)

Continue to use school and community resources.

Meet regularly with your school counselor to discuss your transcript, credits and your plan for senior year. Ask teachers for letters of recommendation and utilize Naviance. Help yourself during senior year by attending Summer Seniors to develop personal goals for your final year and by going to 12th grade family night.

Extend community involvement.

Assume a leadership role in your favorite club, organization or team. Serve others.

In your senior year, try to stay focused on your ultimate goal: college. Doing research and filling out forms may seem boring, but it's essential for getting what you want.

Prepare for your transition to college by using this checklist.
- ☐ Have some scholarship applications ready to submit or already submitted.
- ☐ Visit some colleges; tour their campuses.
- ☐ Pick specific colleges that you want to attend after graduating high school.
- ☐ Update your resume.
- ☐ Get three to four letters of recommendation from your teachers, counselors, coaches, religious leaders or community advisors.
- ☐ Apply to colleges and be mindful of deadlines.
- ☐ Apply for scholarships and be mindful of deadlines.
- ☐ Apply for Free Application for Federal Student Aid (FAFSA) and College Scholarship Service Profile (CSS Profile) by January 1.
- ☐ Submit your deposit to your chosen college.

Scholarship Qualifications

Scholarship qualifications can often be frustrating to sift through. The region you live in, what you want to study in school and even your special interests can all be a part of specific qualifications for various scholarships. Although this is the case, many scholarships share a set of basic eligibility requirements. Meeting these requirements is a key step to getting the kinds of scholarships that you want. The following is a list of basic eligibility qualifications that many scholarships ask for:

- **GPA:** A 3.5+ grade point average (GPA) is standard for many scholarships. The higher your grades, the more scholarships you are likely to be eligible for. However...
- **A Low GPA is Not the End of the World:** However, having a lower GPA does not disqualify you from scholarships. A 2.5 GPA, when accompanied by community service and solid essays, will often be rewarded.
- **Service Work:** Many scholarships fund individuals who get involved in their community. Consistently working at one place shows dedication and is better than being involved in a lot of different community services or organizations.
- **Self-Evaluation:** Understanding yourself and your needs will help you develop positive learning habits. It will also help you write a great personal statement.
- **Strong and Personalized Letters of Recommendation:** Aim for three to four letters — two from teachers, one from a counselor and one more from someone like a service program director, but *not* from a family member.
- **Build Relationships:** Being able to build relationships with other people can increase your opportunities for finding scholarship resources, internships and potential references.
- **Be Well-Rounded:** Most scholarship readers prefer students who not only succeed in academics but in life as well. Focusing only on your academics can limit your ability to apply for some of the scholarships that require volunteer hours or in-school activities.
- **Be Articulate:** This is one of the most important qualities when applying for scholarships. An eloquent, well-spoken essay can get you much farther than one that is difficult or unpleasant to read.
- **Extracurriculars:** Getting involved in school sports, clubs and organizations will show that you are active and willing to put in effort, which is a good way to stand out among the crowd.

Notes

Aim to work on one scholarship a week throughout your senior year.

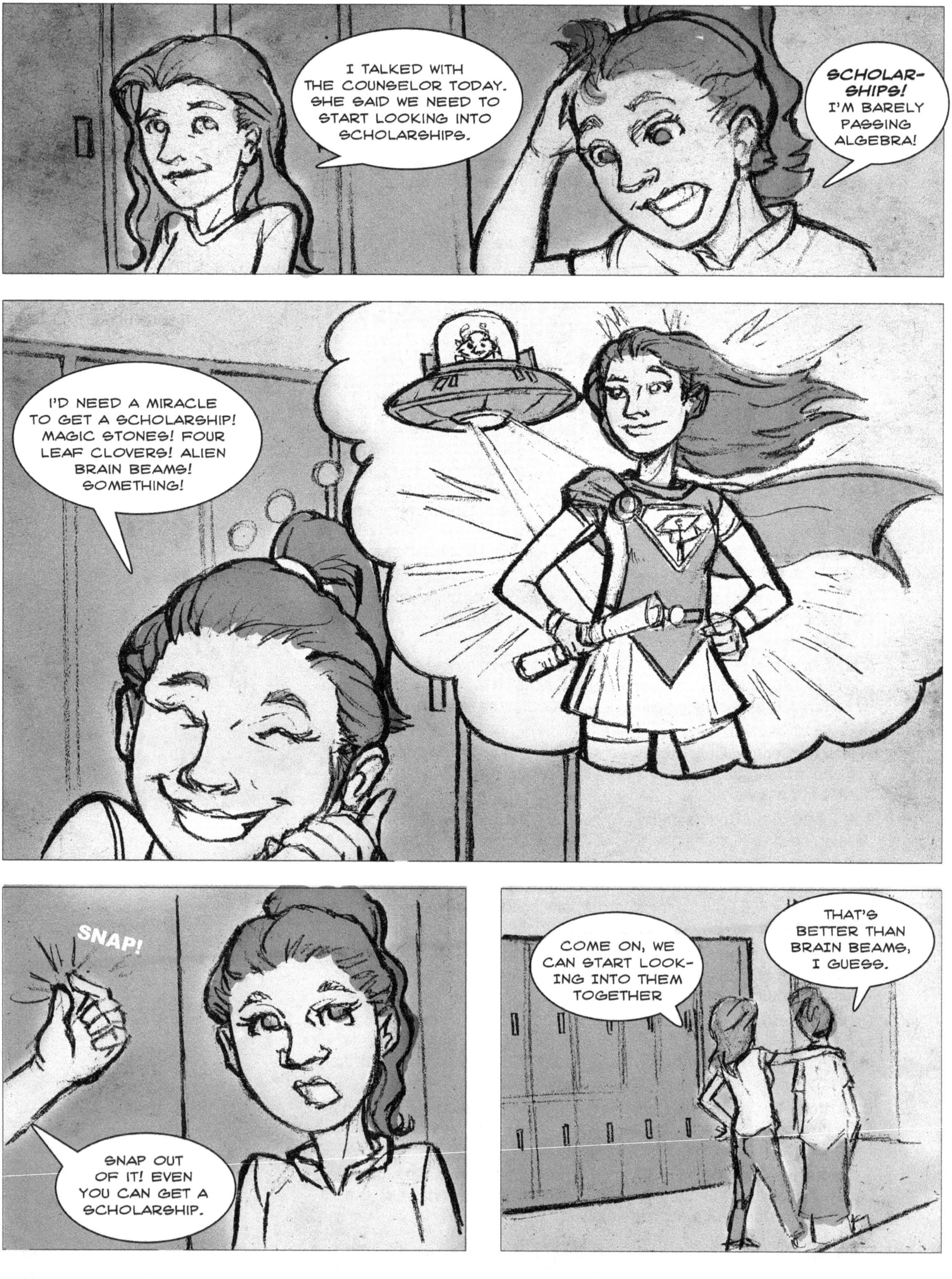

Tackling the Scholarship

By Jocelyn Loyd and Andriana Alexis

Scholarships are a grand way to pay for college. Whether you opt for a full ride or a handful of partial scholarships, both start with the application process. Some colleges receive thousands of scholarship applicants a year. It's up to you to make yourself stand out from the others. You need to be your own promoter. Even if you're the most humble pie in the bakery, this is not the time to sell youself short..

Take Time on the Scholarship Application

There's really no need to be Speedy Gonzalez when handling the application that could literally be the difference between getting into your ideal college for free and not going at all – no pressure. You don't need to take a lifetime filling out the application, but just remember that it's another representation of you. In the end, you could write an incredible essay, submit flattering recommendations and turn in an impressive activity list, but you'll be wallowing in grief if you are rejected for missing a few application questions. So go easy on yourself, don't swallow it whole. Take the application one bite at a time.

Digest the Essay Prompt

Some people race through the essay questions like they're playing Super Mario Kart. Whether or not you're in a time crunch, it's vital to make sure you actually understand what they want from you. You can write the greatest essay ever about your school spirit, but the quality of the essay means absolutely nothing if you've missed the topic. Reread the prompt several times. In fact, it may even dislodge memories worth highlighting.

Be Selective of Content

Even if you're the supreme ruler of an underground mutant kingdom, you do not need to list everything you've done since the dawn of time. Review your activity sheet (or resume) and chalk up key points for your piece. Then you won't have to write blindly for hours on end just to find out you have to start over from scratch. Consider making a goal to only include accomplishments that are relevant to the scholarship prompt, that are important to you and that give you enough to talk about. It sure is cool that in middle school you went to summer camp, but it would be much better to include the time you volunteered at your estranged great uncle's nonprofit organization. No matter what you settle on, never forget to write about what you learned, how you benefited from it and why it's a key activity. Sometimes it's not just *what* you chose, but *why* you chose it.

For example: "I served as a group leader for Outdoor School for two years. It was one of the highlights of my high school years. I helped young 6th graders learn more about nature and their surroundings. It gave me valuable leadership experience and forced me to problem solve for youth with very different personalities and experiences."

Focus, Focus, Focus

We can guarantee you that every scholarship essay you come across will have a word limit. It's crucial that you make sure every word counts. (Check your word count frequently.) Some people tend to ramble and go on long tangents that make absolutely no sense, so the reader ends up not knowing where you're going. When you are only allowed 500 words, it's smarter to focus on a few highlights with great details versus a great number of highlights with few details.

Don't Just Tell

What you say can make you look good, but how you say it will make all the difference. Don't just write "Last summer I was an intern at the Douglas Law Firm. I gained many communication and leadership skills. It was a great experience." Sounds blander than grandma's cold oatmeal, right? There are many ways to spice things up. I know you've

Notes

heard of adjectives – at least I hope so. Here's what the right sensory words can do: "Last summer I was one of a chosen few dedicated interns at the influential Douglas Law Firm. I had to write clear emails to our clients and I wrote case summaries for our lawyers. In the process I also learned how to share my ideas with the lawyers in the firm. It was a life-changing experience." Now it's a bit livelier, wouldn't you say? It makes the reader want to know more about why your experience at the firm was so life changing and why what you learned was so essential. Pick the right words and you'll be in business.

Know the deadlines, and allow enough time to get things done by the due date.

Use Your Own Words

It's often tempting to quote the great men and women of history, but keep in mind that they weren't applying for financial aid when they said all those wonderful things (so go easy on the quoting). We don't need to give you the plagiarism talk, but many find it hard to crank out a thoughtful and original scholarship essay. Some assume if they pepper their piece with the words of likable and/or recognizable figures it will make them a winner. The reason why scholarships include essays isn't just to make your senior year even harder. These essays allow them to see beyond your high school transcript. It gives them a better sense of who is applying. It helps them decide whether or not you deserve financial aid more than the others. Again, no pressure.

Be Yourself

Some students shy away from scholarships because they doubt their accomplishments. They hear about the thespian/volunteer/athlete/student body president/valedictorian who won the big bucks. Never quit before you even start. Many students demonstrate their best qualities in very ordinary activities. "Three days a week I take care of my three siblings after school. I am both patient and firm with them, and I help them with their reading and other homework." If you're excited about something you did, make the scholarship committee excited about it, too. Don't forget to add your own personal touches. If you're funny, then be hilarious. If you're poetic, then make them feel it. Have fun. There's nothing wrong with being original.

Revise! Revise! Revise!

It's worth finding one or two individuals to look over your essays. You are not your own audience. Board members, volunteers, employees of the organization and many other individuals review scholarships. A fresh pair of eyes on your essay will give you an opportunity to receive feedback from a different perspective that can provide insight on information that is unclear or incomplete. Sometimes we spend so much time on a single piece of work that we grow numb to it and can't see the opportunities for revision right in front of our face. Having your essay revised can help catch the things you miss and create a better essay all around. Using a Writing Center or participating in scholarship workshops can help provide those necessary fresh eyes. Don't forget to use spell-check and/or look up words in the dictionary. Use a thesaurus if you find yourself using the same word over and over.

No Scholarship? Get a Grant

The Oregon Opportunity Grant (OOG) is Oregon's largest state-funded need-based grant program for students planning to go to college. These grants are funded primarily by Oregon taxpayers. Every year 10 to 15 Roosevelt students receive these funds. (For more information: www.oregonstudentaid.gov/oregonopportunitygrant.aspx)

If you plan to attend an Oregon state university or community college, you may be able to get most — or possibly all — of your tuition covered. You meet the criteria for the OOG grant if you:

- Are an Oregon resident and a U.S. citizen or eligible non-citizen. (Out-of-state students who are members of Native American tribes with traditional ties to Oregon may be considered Oregon residents.)
- Are an undergraduate student with no prior baccalaureate degrees.

- Plan to be enrolled at least as a half-time student (i.e., at least 6 credit hours) at a participating Oregon-based postsecondary institution.
- Have financial need. Only students with student/family adjusted gross incomes at or below $70,000 are considered for the grant.
- Have no defaults on federal student loans and owe no refunds on federal student grants.
- Have not been incarcerated.

If you meet these requirements, complete the Free Application for Federal Student Aid (FAFSA) by February 1. The FAFSA is the application for most federal student aid programs. Students must complete a FAFSA each year to ensure access to both federal programs and the grants and scholarships that the Oregon Student Assistance Commission (OSAC) administers.

> OSAC gets lots of applications for its grants. To stand out from the crowd, try to be unique and memorable.

Fix FAFSA errors right away!

An email arrives about three days after filing the FAFSA. After five days, check the FAFSA website to confirm it was submitted correctly. If the Student Aid Report (SAR) shows errors or if FAFSA information needs to be corrected, students should resolve those errors right away. Funds are limited, so those who wait too long to resolve errors may not receive a grant. The most common errors are missing signatures and conflicts between a student's name and social security number.

Students do not have to wait until they file a tax return to submit a FAFSA. They can submit a FAFSA using an estimate of their taxable income based on the previous year. After the tax return is filed, students must go online and update their FAFSA record with actual income and other information.

When to apply for an Oregon Opportunity Grant

The Office of Student Access and Completion (OSAC) encourages applicants to submit their FAFSAs by February 1 to ensure priority consideration. Opportunity Grants are awarded on a first-come, first-served basis by application date until funds are depleted. Each spring, OSAC makes awards and notifies students by email of their potential grant eligibility. To ensure receipt of future email notifications from OSAC and from the U.S. Department of Education, students should make sure they include an active email address on their FAFSA.

Sometimes, students who are awarded grant funds but delay enrollment until later in the academic year may lose eligibility. Awards for students who are enrolled half-time in fall term may be limited to half-time amounts for all subsequent terms during the academic year.

Currently, a fixed and renewable award up to $2,100 will be available for full-time, full-year attendance at any eligible Oregon-based postsecondary institution. When this amount is accompanied with federal aid, students who attend Oregon state universities and community colleges can often cover most of their tuition costs. Students' tuition and books costs must be at or above $2,000 per year to be considered for an award. OSAC will release a portion of the award to the student's school account at the start of each academic term.

Federal Pell Grants

A Federal Pell Grant is another grant that, unlike a loan, does not have to be repaid. The maximum Pell grant is usually around $5,775 per 12-month period. The amount you receive depends on your financial need, costs to attend school, status as a full-time or part-time student and plans to attend school for a full academic year or less.

What About Student Loans?

Student loans are another way to finance college, and many students use them. Unlike scholarships and grants, however, a student loan must be repaid to the institution — federal or private — that gave it to you. The repayment includes interest on top of the original loan amount, so the total you owe is higher than the amount you borrowed. For many students, this is a huge burden that lasts long after college. Loans can be very helpful, but know what you are getting into. Research student loans carefully. (For more information: https://studentaid.ed.gov/sa/types/loans)

Successful Scholarship Essays

Notes

A good way to learn how to write scholarship essays is to learn by example. In this section you'll find real essays written by students that were successful in getting the authors scholarships. Because these are the actual essays, they are only lightly edited, so there may be a few grammar and punctuation errors. Look past them to get to the heart of the essays. However, *when writing your essay, be sure to check your spelling and grammar, by using a spell-checker and/or looking it up in the dictionary.*

Accompanying the essays are comments written by students in Roosevelt's AVID (Advancement Via Individual Determination) class. They answered three questions: what they liked about the essay, why they thought it was successful and how they could use it as inspiration for their own scholarship essays. *To see which sentences stood out and captured AVID students' attention, look for text in the essays that are highlighted in bold italic type.*

Portland State University Diversity Scholarship

Linnette Meshack (RHS 2013)
Warner Pacific and Portland Community College
Linnette will major in either social work or business. She received the full-ride ACT Six Leadership scholarship. She is very passionate about pursuing higher education.

Essay Prompt: *Imagine: You are a Service Learning project coordinator. Please describe a service learning project you would coordinate. Why did you choose this project? How would you get others involved in the service learning opportunity? (400 word limit)*

My community service project would be to create a non-profit organization called I Care. I Care would be an organization that is meant to help the homeless. The way it would work is to get a box and fill it with essential needs such as food, water and other things, like a blanket, new socks, a pair of gloves, a hat, and a scarf. ***Also included in the box would be a heart-felt letter explaining why it's important to never lose hope and to inform them that there are people in this world that do care.*** Also provided in the box would be an envelope with a stamp already on it and writing materials, in hopes that they would write the organization back to let us know how the I Care package helped them or better yet changed their lives. The box would be hand-delivered by a group of youth accompanied by an adult to show the community that today's youth does care. I chose this project because every day on my way to and from school I pass through downtown Portland and I always see a homeless person. I've seen a man sleeping on the cold, hard, wet ground with no blanket, sleeping bag, no socks or shoes and it breaks my heart. ***The way I would get others involved would be to look for members in the community who share my passion in helping people who are less fortunate.***

Essay Prompt: *Given your personal background, describe an experience that illustrates what you would bring to the diversity at Portland State University? (400 word limit)*

Diversity is so broad that it can be interpreted in so many different ways. It's a range of different things that are not limited to gender, race, and culture. Diversity means to act, look or have unique qualities that are different from the majority of

similar people or things. I attend a very diverse high school that is located in a non-diverse city. Everyday I walk down the halls of Roosevelt High School I come in contact with multiple races of students who come from a huge range of different backgrounds. Many of my fellow classmates speak more than one language. Even my closest friends are a different race and come from a different culture and religion than me. One of my best friends identifies herself as black and Native American and my other best friend identifies herself as white and Native American. ***Having friends that are different than me opens my eyes to realize that everyone is not the same and that's okay.*** Their stories, culture and background interest me. ***Coming from a diverse high school has help me learn the importance of what it means to love people for who they are and to know that my friends don't have to look like me.*** I've learned how to not be prejudiced or judgmental. I think diversity is very important because if we all looked the same and came from the same place and believe in the same things, life would be boring

> Don't just tell people what you think. Show your point of view with specific examples. Describe your experience and how it affected you.

 Do you think these essays are successful? Why?
- "This is a successful essay because she uses a lot of descriptive language and she makes sure she shows us her ideas and opinions, rather than to just tell us."
- "What makes this essay successful is how the author writes out her plan for something she wants to do for others. Also she explains what diversity means to her and what she thinks about it. The paragraphs are pretty strong, especially the last line of the second paragraph. I don't think I could have ever found a better way to end a diversity essay than that line."

 What did you learn from this essay that will help you with your own scholarship application?
- "I can make my own winning essay by describing what diversity means to me and writing about how I'm diverse. I would chunk down the paragraphs because I feel like they are too big. Another thing I would take from this essay is to find a good ending line like the author did."

Future Connect Scholarship

Tanya Tirado-Ramirez
Portland Community College
Tanya will major in criminal justice so she can become a positive symbol for her community. She is passionate about playing soccer. She is proud to be a Chicana, especially since she gets to be a part of two different cultures.

Essay Prompt: *Explain your career aspirations and your educational plan to meet these goals. Be specific about how enrolling at PCC will help you reach your goals. (500 word maximum please)*

I want you to look at me as a role model, one of your heroes. I want to major in Criminal Justice and become a police officer. ***It takes motivation, bravery, a positive attitude and the ability to take risks.*** It seems like a lot to do, but it's part of my dream and I won't give up no matter what. My role will be to protect my community. I will also go to schools to talk to the students so I can tell them to stay in school and not make mistakes by dropping out or choosing the wrong path. Instead of deciding to do drugs, I will encourage them to get involved in a sport or an activity they enjoy. This dream will come true if I stay on task, continue with school and take the necessary classes to learn how to defend others and myself. ***I plan to stick with all my goals and not let anything slip through my hands.***

Essay Prompt: *Describe a significant accomplishment or challenge you faced in the last 5 years. What did you learn about yourself from this experience? (500 word maximum please)*

Even though I was born here I was brought to Mexico as a little child because my mom wanted my little sister Brenda and I to meet our grandparents. We lived there for three years. The learning method I used was unorthodox. *I was born here, but it didn't help my English very much. It has been hard to manage two languages (English and Spanish) when you live in two different worlds.* On my soccer team all the girls just spoke English. I tried to communicate with them, but it was very difficult. I was afraid to talk to them because I didn't want them to make fun of my accent. Every day was a challenge; I discovered new words that I tried to learn so that one day I could use them. I am rich in two special cultures — Mexican and American. *To be a better person, there are challenges you need to overcome in life to get to the other level of your life.*

One summer day I was walking with my friends when they decided to join the soccer team from school. When I came the first day of practice I was terrified because my coach looked very strict. I couldn't think of something else, but just smile at her. I started in Junior Varsity. I wasn't sad because I was playing my favorite sport, and to be a professional soccer player takes time. The first game was on a sunny Tuesday. I did pretty well. The next day after practice my coach called me over. I walked towards her. She looked at me and said "be ready, you are playing for Varsity tomorrow." I couldn't believe it. I thought it was going to be just one game, but I stayed there the whole season. At the end I received a plaque for Most Improved Player. I was so proud of myself.

There is often a point in life where you need to give up a passion to help your family. I used to play soccer every Saturday in the morning. One day I got home, and my dad told me that he wasn't going to be able to pay my phone bill anymore. I said why? He said "I only have one job I can't afford it." He said, "If you want to keep your phone you have to work." I immediately said yes and started looking for a job. The only day available was Saturdays; *I then realized it was either soccer or job.* I cried the first days. It was frustrating, but when I got my first check all the hard work of getting up early and missing games was worth it. I started helping my parents with things for the house.

> *Stating a personal belief can be very powerful.*

Do you think this essay is successful? Why?

- "Tanya's essay may have occasional spelling or grammar mistakes, but it more than makes up for it with consistently asserting her will and determination to improve and not ever give up. She shows growth and development with the difficulties she has faced and comes off as a reliable, upstanding person."
- "Even though her essay had spelling and grammar mistakes she didn't let that set her back from applying for the scholarship and the mistakes actually show her determination to improve and not give up."

What did you learn from this essay that will help you with your own scholarship application?

- "When writing my own scholarship application, I should talk not only about how I have struggled, but how I've learned from the struggles I've faced and how they drive my goals and make me a better person, which is something that the author of this essay did well."

Peninsula Optimist Club Scholarship

Stephanie Martinez (RHS 2013)
Portland Community College
Stephanie is an ambitious student who wants to positively impact her community. She strives to do so by becoming an F.B.I. agent.

Notes

Essay Prompt: *Write a personal essay describing your career goal(s) and education plan. (Two pages maximum)*

Sitting in my office I get a call from my fellow Federal Bureau of Investigation agent saying that we are going to Florida because there is a serial killer on the loose. ***This is how I picture myself in the future since my goal is to go to college and major in Criminal Justice with a focus on being an F.B.I. agent.*** One day, I would like to be at a crime scene investigation, figuring out what happened and who the criminals are. I would love to help families find relief and hope by finding those who caused, or are causing, harm to their loved ones. So far, I have been volunteering and working with both children and the elderly by involving myself in the community. I have volunteered in an elementary school as a mentor and with an after school program called Schools Uniting Neighborhoods. I look forward to serving the community through my future role as an officer and community member.

I am not letting my past affect my educational needs of becoming someone with a career. So far, I know I want to get my Bachelors of Science in Criminal Justice. My current adopted family has always said that no matter what, education always comes first. My parents constantly tell me, "Better yourself and become the person who your real parents were not able to be." This is another reason why I want to better myself and inspire my future. Both of my current parents dropped out of elementary school in Mexico, I want to attend college to make them proud. Once I graduate High School, I plan on attending Portland Community College for two years and earning my transfer degree. For the last two years of my major, I will attend Western Oregon University and be a part of their Criminal Justice program. I would love to get involved in some volunteering with the local F.B.I. or police department. This would help me gain more one-on-one experience for what I will be doing in the future. ***I plan on attending college to get my degree and give back to the community as a criminal investigator. Getting the Peninsula Optimist Scholarship would put me one step closer to achieving my goal.***

> Face the scholarship head on. Say how it will help you achieve your goals.

Do you think this essay is successful? Why?

- "She mentioned what motivated her but didn't just blankly say it. Instead, she showed it through quotes from her adopted family. She told the audience why the scholarship would benefit her and why she deserved it."

- "This essay was successful because of how she foreshadowed in the beginning of her essay, instead of just stating it so blatantly. She then talked about what she did to prepare for what job she wanted to do in the future."

- "What makes this essay successful is the motivation it has within every line written. The author of this essay describes a very personal topic in her writing — her past. One of the things that makes an essay successful is getting personal. I personally think this student did a good job in addressing that part."

- "The fact that the student already has a plan for what she wants to do after high school makes it successful because she is showing more than just a plan."

- "'As I sit in my office I get a call from my fellow F.B.I. agent saying that we are going to Florida because there is a serial killer on the loose.' This essay puts the audience right in the scene the author has for them. You can feel the emotion of the person that wrote this essay."

What did you learn from this essay that will help you with your own scholarship application?

- "Since I already have my plan for what I want to do after high school, I can include that in my essays. Lastly, I would probably consider writing a little bit more about my motivations."

César E. Chávez Leadership Conference Scholarship

Darlene Munoz-Valle (RHS 2013)
Portland State University
Darlene is an active community member who strives to make the environment around her a better place for all.

Essay Prompt: *Tell us about your educational goals and what steps you have taken to reach your career goal. How will this scholarship help you reach your college education goals? (250 words or less)*

    I had the opportunity to be alongside my mother when she was having a C-section. The whole process and the excitement of seeing the doctor take out my baby sister made me realize what I wanted to do with my life. There are no words to describe the emotions I felt seeing this beautiful baby for the first time. I was brave; I had seen blood and the placenta while I watched the doctor cut open my mom's stomach. **I realized my destiny is to be a Nurse Midwife. I want to work in South America where they are in more need than we are.** Watching my grandmother, who was in Mexico at the time, get denied health care because she didn't have the money made me want to help all those people who might not be able to receive the same health care. I don't only want to study for midwifery; I want to be the one who helps the less fortunate. I've already been accepted to a four-year university; that's a step closer in pursuing my dreams. I will pursue a degree in pre-nursing. **I am the future and my motivation to succeed comes from those who need me. Now nothing can stop me, as I'm more motivated than ever. By winning this scholarship, I will have more money to pursue college.**

> Be confident. Say who you are, what you want and why. Show that you are motivated.

Essay Prompt: *What has been the most significant lesson you have learned from your involvement in leadership, community service, work experience, or extracurricular activities? (250 words or less)*

    Step Up has been a big part of my life, as it has played an important role in my life since my freshman year. It all started off as a commitment to attend Step Up, which is an after-school mentoring program that focuses on helping incoming ninth graders transition into high school successfully. I have continued to stick with Step Up now for my fourth year even though it's not a requirement. **Step Up has helped me build bridges between family and school, and a consistent support system that has made me a stronger person, full of determination and goals.** It has also made me a more mature and responsible person and has provided opportunities to visit colleges. I've learned to take things slower and to be more patient, because things will come to us at the right moment. **Step Up has shown me that we are not alone and that there is always going to be someone to give you support.** As a senior I have received a lot of support from my advocate. My classmates and I also give support to each other as we write essays for scholarships.

Essay Prompt: *What has been the biggest obstacle you have overcome (or are working to overcome) and what did you learn from it (or are learning)? (250 words or less)*

    Tears roll down my face, that salty taste goes into my mouth. My mom gave me one really tight hug. I usually say no to those hugs because I feel uncomfortable and shy, but this hug was full of love and pain. With one single hug, she transmitted all of her sadness. I then realized my mother was not okay and there were problems. From the point when my mother found out she had a tumor to the day she got surgery, we never lost our faith. Problems stacked up as my mother stayed more in bed and had more appointments. **Cleaning before leaving for school and coming home on time to make dinner for my family put a lot of pressure on my shoulders.** I was so busy thinking about what could happen and all of my problems, which got in the way of my education. The day of the surgery was tense. I stayed

> Go ahead: get personal. Let them see what makes you tick.

home with my brother instead of attending school, and I cried so much while praying to God for a miracle. Today my mother is alive and I thank God every morning for this blessing. *From this obstacle I transformed into a leader.* I am appreciative and I never lose faith because God is with us.

Essay Prompt: *The theme of the 25th Anniversary of the CECLC is, "Look how far we've come." As a student getting ready to graduate from high school, how do you relate the theme and César E. Chavez's legacy to your own personal story? (250 words or less)*

From César Chávez I learned to fight with intelligence, not violence. César Chávez taught me to think smart and act smart. If you're an immigrant or whatever race you are, don't be afraid of showing who you really are. We came here because we were told that this is the country where we can live our dreams, "Sueño Americano." Immigrants keep coming here to succeed in life, but then there's injustice and discrimination towards them. They come here to do the labor jobs that native-born Americans are not willing to do for low pay. I never knew how hard it was until I experienced it myself. Working in agriculture is not an easy job. By the end of my first day I had only made twenty dollars. I know that I should show respect to these people; knowing how hard it is and only making enough to live for the day makes me think how hard it is for those who have a family to support. They need to raise their voices because what they receive is not a living wage. *Everybody's voice counts and you don't need to be a certain age or have enough money to be heard and to make a change. I am not César Chávez, I am Darlene Munoz. I, too, believe that with my voice, I can make a difference in this world.*

> Be optimistic. Speak positively about yourself and your future.

Do you think this essay is successful? Why?
→ "Something the writer of this essay did well was clearly outline her goals and emphasize her dedication to accomplishing them. You really got the sense that she was driven to succeed."

What did you learn from this essay that will help you with your own scholarship application?
→ "When I write my essay, I should make the reader understand that I'm motivated by my goals and talk about my motivations for those goals."

Kaiser Permanente Health Care Career Scholarship

Darlene Munoz-Valle (RHS 2013)

Essay Prompt: *Why are you interested in your chosen health care profession? What have you done to research a career in this field (e.g. job shadowing, internship, interviewing professionals in the field)?*

I had the opportunity to be alongside my mother when she was having a C-section. The whole process and the excitement of seeing the doctor take out my baby sister made me realize what I wanted to do with my life. There are no words to describe the emotions I felt seeing this beautiful baby for the first time. I was brave: I had seen blood, the placenta and the doctor cut open my mom's stomach. I realized my destiny is to be a midwife. *I don't only want to study for midwifery; I want to be the one who helps the less fortunate.* Babies are my passion and I have had a lot of experience with them, as I have babysat newborn babies and taken good care of them.

Junior year I signed up to take Health and Science class, and there I learned all about how a nurse should treat their patients and basic medical instruments. Throughout the year we learned how to take our pulse rates, use the stethoscope and use the blood pressure monitor. I also took Anatomy and Physiology. I learned all the names of the body muscles. I actually struggled in the class as I didn't receive enough support from

> It's OK to re-use parts of an essay for a different scholarship, as long as it answers the prompt. In fact, it makes sense to be consistent and efficient.

my teacher. I personally enjoyed that class a lot, though, and learned so much about the structure of the body and how it worked. I've recently been introduced to a nurse practitioner, she has introduced herself and I have gotten to know her. *I'm so interested in learning more about her career because nursing and helping others is really meaningful to me.* I have also recently been in contact with a midwife who is really good friends with a tutor from my school. I'm really excited in getting to know more of her experience and hopefully I will soon have the chance to do a job shadowing with her so I can have my own experience.

Essay Prompt: *Tell us about a high school teacher who has been an inspiration to you. What is the teacher's name and the school where he or she teaches or taught you? How did this teacher make an impact on your life? (Limit: 800 characters with spaces)*

"You're a smart girl and there is nothing too hard if you set your mind to it. I believe in you and you, too, have to believe in yourself." Even if she is in the worst mood, she never shows it, instead leaves her problems behind and smiles. Mrs. Strom, my pre-calculus teacher who works at Roosevelt High School, always makes sure to be showing with pride that she is a Rough Rider. *She has inspired and has made me believe in myself, to never let myself down and not leave things to "what if." She pushes me to continue in a way so that I don't feel pressured but a desire to continue fighting and not give up.* There are times when school gets hard or, even in her class, I get confused or fail her tests. She tells me that instead of being disappointed in myself, show myself what I am capable of doing. With her patience, support and words of advice, she has shown who I truly am and that I am capable of doing what I set my mind to.

Beat the Odds Scholarship

Rachel Kelley (RHS 2012)
Portland State University
Rachel is a full-time student at Portland State University.

Essay Prompt: *Please describe the most significant adversities or challenge(s) you have faced in life. How have you overcome these adversities/ challenges? How have these challenge(s) shaped your character? How have you grown as a result?*

To put it simply, my family never had money and always ended up with the short end of the stick. My parents both worked low-income jobs; my mother worked as a caretaker at a nursing home and my father was a parking lot painter. I didn't grow up with a lot of the opportunities that my peers did. I usually went to work with one parent or the other, because we couldn't afford a babysitter. At times we didn't have enough money to pay our bills, so our electricity and water would often get shut off. I would have to go without showers and use the neighbor's bathroom, or my parents would have me stay at a friend's house.

On December 8th, 2005, just two days after my mom's 48th birthday, she had a stroke. She had pneumonia and coughed too hard, breaking a blood vessel in her brain. My brother was the one who found her on the floor, and my dad was the one who called 911. This took quite a toll on my family. It was unimaginably heart breaking to wait in the hospital for eight hours wondering whether or not my mom would be coming home. She survived, but the left side of her body shut down and her mind is still on the road to recovery. During the three months my mother was in the hospital, we had to completely rearrange our house to fit her needs. We had to build a ramp so we could get her in and out of the house. Since my mom couldn't take care of the household anymore, I had to do it and take care of her along with staying motivated to excel in school. *This unexpected incident forced me to have to grow up very quickly. Luckily, I had my family's support through all the hardships I faced.*

Over the years her mind has improved and she keeps herself busy with television, reading books, doing small art projects and trips to the store. *I decided that if my life right*

> Be direct. Stay on topic. Make sure the entire essay relates to the prompt.

now was going to be hard, I was going to work my hardest so when I get older I won't have to struggle as much as my parents did. School became my number one priority. I couldn't stand missing a single day of school. My body told me I needed to be there and I had a hunger for learning. When being home was hard, I looked to school for comfort. I wanted something that made me happy and succeeding in school fulfilled this need, and that's what I focused on.

> Be real.

One skill that I have acquired over the years is the desire to help people. Whether it is through fundraisers or helping someone work through a tough situation, I love helping others. I think this was greatly influenced from taking care of my mom for the last six years. It has helped me to develop skills in caring for others. After I graduate high school I plan to go to college so that I can become a counselor. I plan to help other children and teens through tough situations and struggles that they may be going through in their own lives. I want to show them that focusing on school will help open doors that they could never imagine. *When I was younger, I could never imagine that a kid like me, growing up so far below the poverty line in North Portland and the St. Johns community, would even be able to consider going to college.*

Do you think this essay is successful? Why?

→ "What makes this essay successful is that she had a great hook. By reading the first line it made me want to keep reading and know more about her life. What I can take from this essay is how she actually told us about how she had to deal with things that she didn't have. I noticed that I have many connections with her, too."

→ "This essay is successful because she answered the prompt directly. There were multiple reasons why she beat the odds of her life but they all were similar and she connected them."

→ "Her first paragraph was really strong it hooked and moved the reader. This essay wasn't complex, but it was simple and detailed to get the point across."

What did you learn from this essay that will help you with your own scholarship application?

→ "What I can take from this essay is how to have a strong beginning and make the reader know how I feel or felt. Don't try make to the complex be simple, but make sure it is understandable."

Essay Prompt: *Please reflect on the lesson(s) you have learned from your volunteer service or leadership experience. What are some important lessons you have learned?*

When I'm not in school, I am involved in a variety of activities. *After school I am part of a group called GSA, which stands for Gay Straight Alliance. I am an ally and I wholeheartedly believe in equality between all people.* I believe that the LGBTQ community should be treated with the same respect as any other community member. We participate in No-Name-Calling Week to raise awareness about respecting others and that "being gay" is not an insult.

During the summer I am in a program called 4-H which stands for hands, heart, head and health. 4-H is a positive youth development organization that empowers young people to reach their full potential. 4-H enables America's youth to emerge as leaders through hands-on learning. These programs are research-based and adult mentorships that give back to their local communities. *I raise goats and show them at the Klickitat County Fair during the summer in Goldendale, Washington.* All summer long I stay with my grandparents working hard with my goats, memorizing information and learning new ways to better my learning experience while on the farm.

I also volunteer at my grandparents' church helping run a program called Vacation Bible School to teach children about God. I am in charge of the puppet shows, organizing the games, teaching lessons in the classroom and helping just about everywhere I'm needed, including assisting in setting up yard sales to raise funds for the program. During the holiday season, I volunteer at the Optimist Club Tree Lot getting trees ready to sell and sometimes delivering them directly to houses. *I have also helped the last two years in organizing concerts to raise money for Haiti. Soon after the devastating earthquake, my peers and I were motivated to help others in need. We even continued to support the cause after people stopped helping.*

Essay Prompt: *Is there any other information you would like us to know that may be helpful in considering your scholarship application?*

Overall I can say that I am grateful for all of the hardships I have faced in my life. *Living in poverty has built me into a more resilient person, and my mom having a stroke has given me the ability to apply that strength into a career as a counselor.* I will be able to share with others who have hard lives a real life example of what can be accomplished, even through the toughest of situations.

Gates Millennium Scholarship

Warren Vang (RHS 2013)
Oregon State University
Warren is going to major in biochemistry and biophysics. He looks forward to meeting other students at OSU who want to succeed in life.

Essay Prompt: *Discuss the subjects in which you excel or have excelled. To what factors do you attribute your success? Use specific examples to illustrate how you succeeded. (Responses from 600-1,000 words preferred)*

A hundred faces stared forward in anticipation, waiting for the verdict. Heart pounding, thump, thump, thump. I could feel my anxiousness growing exponentially. Today would be judgment day; the day when I would be condemned to be invisible forever or the day when others learned my name. My heart continued to beat faster and faster, showing no sign of stopping. The announcer read off the names of the students who were chosen, and with each name my fear overshadowed my confidence. She came to the "Expository Essay" category, began to read a paragraph and spoke the words: "With such a huge victory they completely decimated and annihilated one of the most magnificent civilizations that once existed." It was then I knew what the verdict was.

> Capture their attention with a strong introduction.

I have always been told that freshman year is the most important year of one's high school experience. When I got my first essay assignment, I was frightened by the length that our teacher required it to be. *Staring down at that white piece of paper, reading over the directions and how it had to be structured was overwhelming. I never considered myself a good writer because no one ever said I was.* Although we spent many weeks beforehand researching and analyzing the impact of the novel *Guns, Germs and Steel* on the development of technology, I had no idea how I was going to piece the evidence together. Whenever I could, I put the assignment aside, procrastinated doing work on it and drove myself to madness. I kept thinking to myself, "This essay has to be good because if it's not, teachers won't ever look at my writing the same way again." Ultimately, that way of thinking enlightened me and turned on the switch inside my head.

Writing an outline of my essay at that point seemed effortless. I went through two versions of an outline: one that was complex, called a tower diagram, and the standard one, called a tree diagram. When I looked at the instructions a second time, I realized that our essay only called for five paragraphs, yet, according to my outline, I was going to write seven. To everyone else, I was either crazy or an overachiever. It was never my intention to write that much, but before I knew it, there it was.

Notes

> Be descriptive. Let them see the scene through your eyes.

As soon as I began writing the rough draft of my essay, it was more than just words and evidence being thrown together; it was the future of my high school education. This was what I wanted teachers to remember me by; the first essay I would write as a high school student.

The final draft ended up totaling to 1,883 words detailing the causes of *Guns, Germs and Steel* and the implications it had on the development of the known world. When I finally received my essay back from my teacher, I was thrilled that I had received one of the highest scores on writing that he gave to any student. My teacher even offered to put my writing on the board. *Although it was nothing more than a light brown, stained cabinet with a laminated white paper that read "Excellent Writing," the recognition was a new experience that I had never felt before.* I had succeeded in proving that I was a good writer, despite what others may have said about me in the past.

My heart rate continued to increase, weighed down by the thought that my writing may not be good enough. I sheltered myself from the announcer with a swing of my backpack. First, I thought about my own controversial issues, like why I turned in my essays to this competition in the first place, knowing that as a freshman there was no possibility of me winning. Nervously, I stared up at the orator reading the paragraph. I listened and carefully analyzed every sentence she enunciated. Nothing seemed to stand out, until she said, "With such a huge victory they completely decimated and annihilated one of the most magnificent civilizations that once existed." I could feel myself calming down, heart rate decreasing and a sigh of relief washed over me. Instead of feeling anxiety, I felt jubilant. Once again I was acknowledged for something no one ever spoke about. However, as much as that moment affected me, what I most felt accomplished about was that writing now became what matched me to my upperclassmen. It labeled me as an individual who was unique and everyone treated me like that from then on.

Writing was always something I believed I failed miserably at because no one ever said otherwise, but I was wrong. As I look back on that experience and realize that I have learned so much about myself. What I attribute to my success in writing is the motivation I received from wanting to be a perfect student. I know that I will never be the best writer, but I am telling my story in a way that makes sense means more to me. *Sadly, I know that I can never be a perfect student, but perhaps I can show that I am more than who I am through my writing.*

Essay Prompt: *Discuss the subjects with which you had difficulties. What factors do you believe contributed to your difficulties? How have you dealt with them so they will not cause problems for you again? In what areas have you experienced the greatest improvement? What problem areas remain? Explain how you identified your problems, and give examples of how you made or attempted to make improvements. (600-1,000 words)*

"All rise, the Federal Court of Oregon is now in session, the Honorable Judge presiding." The clerk rises to a standing position, announces the docket, "Your Honor, today's case involves the State of Oregon Vs. Willy Freeman." I shuddered as a chill ran down my spine as the trial of a lifetime began and my confidence crumbled.

> Hook them in with a statement that makes them want to keep reading.

It all began by chance. As I stared down at a piece of paper that included my name and the list of classes I was enrolled in, one particular class seemed to stand out to me, Judicial Systems. At first I was confused. Had I signed up for this class? On my way to class during a typical B day schedule, I began to notice myself entering an unknown part of the school. Although it had the same white colored walls with its boring repetition of gray lockers and brown doors, it was a hallway that I had never walked down before. Approaching my destination I realized that this was a law class. I had just realized that Judicial stems from one of the main branches of the government and if I remember correctly, it is the branch that interprets the law. *I thought to myself, "What sort of mess have I gotten myself into now?"*

Entering through the threshold of the doorway, I only saw six students seated and ready for class to begin. As the teacher began to speak and describe what Judicial Systems incorporated, I couldn't help but figure out the reason why there were only a handful of students enrolled in this class. When I snapped back to reality, she described a competition that was designed to pit our group of "lawyers" against other local schools. The thought of a competition that majestic scared me. There were three factors to this: the enormous amount of material that had to be memorized beforehand, the thought that I didn't want to be judged for looking stupid in front of strangers and the most influential, my long-term fear of speaking in public.

The majority of the year was spent grinding away at trying to learn the rules of the competition and acting out the parts as perfectly as possible. It was arduous being both a Defense Attorney and a Prosecution Attorney because it meant doing double the work. I had no idea how to act and every time I would speak, my pronunciations of the phrases given to me to memorize always came out stuttered. I was a liability to the group and everyone knew it. However, despite what they knew I was, they always encouraged me to perform at my very best and told me keep trying no matter what. I never liked learning about law before, but somehow that encouragement helped me continue forward.

My heartbeat was accelerating so quickly that it felt like I was going to faint. As I put on my white button up, slipped on my black dress shoes and carefully arranged my striped black and white tie, I couldn't help but feel a chill go up my spine. **My fear of public speech was coming back, unwanted, at the most crucial time that I needed to get myself together. Furiously I reread my lines, trying to memorize them one last time on the bus; the ride felt like a roller coaster of horrors as I was faced with my biggest nightmare.**

The opening statements were read and the jury became locked in an emotionless glare of intimidation. As I stepped up to defend my client, I realized that I had forgotten my lines. I began to feel like I was heating up. The only thing I could think of was finishing my part of the trial as fast as possible. I grabbed my "cheat" sheet, quickly read the questions to the defendant, listened to the response and politely concluded, "That is all your honor." With a sigh of relief, I was greeted with a spot on the brown bench that our team sat on.

Mock trial was a new experience for me. *I was thrown into something I was not ready for, but I learned from the risk of speaking in front of strangers and challenging myself to step outside my comfort zone.* Since then, I have spoken more frequently because I take the opportunities to show the world who I am. *Judicial Systems has made me understand that I shouldn't worry about what others will think of me if I mess up, but that I should worry about what I think of myself.* I think it's funny how law didn't hold my interest for very long, yet it helped me overcome my greatest obstacle in life.

Speaking on behalf of what I am passionate about to various groups such as College Board members at Lewis & Clark College or pitching a proposal to gain partnerships, maybe even discussing the impact that an experience has had on me to students at my school, has made me overcome the initial fear of public speech. *I want to continue to expose myself to opportunities that will test the boundaries of my comfort zone because I want to be a great orator someday.* I know that I have a long way to go before the stuttering stops, but as long as I can be involved in subjects like Judicial Systems that help ease my fears while teaching me something that will be essential in life, then I know that I can do it. *The day that I can stand up for what I believe in and cherish most will be the day I know I achieved something majestic; the day when I will finally break free of my fear of public speaking.*

Do you think this essay is successful? Why?

- "This is successful because it illustrates the problem well and has dialogue that engages the reader. I think it's well structured and it answers the prompt. The conclusion refers back to the prompt and has no loose ends. The essay is also really honest and personal, and I think that makes it more interesting for the reader. It has figurative language and paints pictures of the scenes. Overall, it's really well done and entertaining."

- "What makes this a successful essay is that the introduction is really strong and good. It really catches the readers' attention, wanting the reader to keep reading and finish the essay ... What the writer does well is put the reader in his place, making the writing come alive."

Notes

> Show that you are up for a challenge, that you're not afraid to take risks. Then make sure to state what happened when you did.

What did you learn from this essay that will help you with your own scholarship application?

→ "I want to make sure I have a strong introduction just like this essay, because it is the heart of the essay, and the piece would not function well without one."

QuestBridge National College Match

Warren Vang (RHS 2013)

Essay Prompt: *Tell us about an experience you have had or a concept you have learned about that intellectually excites you. Why does it interest you, and what does this tell us about you? (500 word limit)*

Race, it's still defined by the color of our skin and it is still a vicious societal cycle that one can never escape.

I never noticed race growing up. To me, race never existed until high school, because no one ever racially grinded my gears. ***I may not know what it feels like to be purposely discriminated against, but that doesn't mean that I'm not affected by it.*** Attending Roosevelt has changed my perspective on the social construction of race. Until I hit high school, I never realized how much race actually affected my friends. Whenever someone would ask, "who has been a victim of racial discrimination?", hands would shoot up all around me. I wouldn't raise my hand. I was never a victim of outright discrimination. When it came time to analyze the term race, I was always annoyed because no matter how thoughtful or well articulated the student's arguments were, they always ended back at the same initial argument. Then it became clear, the reason that race is never resolved is because it is the product of society.

Race is difficult to comprehend beneath its color. It's something that has no end and no real beginning. I've been in numerous conversations where students' have given their opinions on where they think the term race originated. I hear an answer such as "something that slave owners created to separate from their property." By hearing that, I wanted to believe it myself because that was primarily what I was taught. But that's not true. What is, however, is that race was not constructed by slave owners, but by years of giving the term power. ***Society constructed race when it needed to build a hierarchy so "elites" could subvert equality.*** By word of mouth, it began to form a meaning; it began to be commonplace in our rhetoric. In modern society, we have sheltered ourselves from the truth.

> Be philosophical. It's OK to say what you think about something.

No one wants to discuss what he or she doesn't fully understand. This is why race interests me. I want to understand race, not just through a societal lens, but scientifically as well. ***By understanding what race really means, I can work towards being a better doctor. I want to be like the doctors that were my role models. I want to promote an environment where race has no meaning when treating a patient***, or developing a cure for any child, adult, or elder. If society knew that 99 percent of our DNA is similar, then maybe their opinions would change. If we continue to give meaningless labels power and prestige, then the labels will continue to define who we are externally. ***I, for one, am not content with living in a future where race is what defines us. That is why I learn, why I fight, why I continue to talk about race and educate my peers on what race really is. What this tells you is that I am willing to fight for a change, one where race won't define who I am.***

 Do you think this essay is successful? Why?

→ "It successfully hooked me in with this amazing hook. The intensity of the hook really got me thinking about what race really is and my question was answered as I read."

- "The essay also had a really good flow of ideas, and I didn't have to stop after each sentence to figure out what the writer was trying to convey."
- "This essay was really successful in the way that it didn't go off topic from the discussion of race. It also has a variety of vocabulary. The thing that I really enjoyed in this essay is that it had a sense of philosophy that really stuck with me."

What did you learn from this essay that will help you with your own scholarship application?
- "Something positive that I can really take from this essay and consider while writing my own scholarship essays is the strong use of words such as "hierarchy" or "subvert." This use of complex words really made the essay go from superficial to deep analysis of what race is."
- "An important thing that I can take away from this essay is to always stay on topic and don't ramble. One other thing is to include some philosophy that'll make my essay sound more interesting."

> Don't ramble. No need to tell your life story unless you've been asked for it.

Bank of America Joe Martin Scholarship

Warren Vang (RHS 2013)

Essay Prompt: *What challenges do you see in your community and how do you see yourself contributing to your proposed solutions for these challenges? (1,000 character maximum)*

Writing has always had a devastating effect on the lives of youths as they progress through life. I try not to recognize the influence that writing has had on my life and the opportunities that have come with it. Up until high school, I hated writing so much. **Combating the negative stigma surrounding writing is more than just acknowledging that the challenge exists.** I see myself making writing interesting. As I have learned, writing for the purposes of a grade will never lead to the most inspirational pieces. ***Instead, I will create opportunities where students can express themselves openly, whether through writing or through speech.*** Much like how I am a Writing Consultant at my school, I want to continue to make students better writers, both now as a high school senior and as an accomplished college student. Being able to suggest changes and spot grammatical errors are what I hope to contribute as a stepping-stone to making this problem less apparent.

Essay Prompt: *Describe a leadership challenge you have encountered and the personal growth you achieved from facing that challenge. (1,000 character maximum)*

The Freedom Riders were rebels, but rebels in the way that they defied the restrictions of the Jim Crow Era. They sacrificed their lives for a cause they knew was right and, in an era that bathed itself in racism, that was a hard thing. Being a Freedom Riders Docent threw me into the leadership role of communicating with the public about an event that I knew very little about.

I remember one of the first conversations I had with a Caucasian man. He told me about how he had just watched the "Freedom Riders" movie on PBS and how terrible it was that people of his race could do such grotesque things and get away with it. I didn't have a response for him then and I'm sure I never will.

Since my involvement with the Historic Black Colleges and Universities group, I have developed a new motivation to succeed and I have learned that I should fight for myself. No one is ever sure of what the future holds and because of that, I want to be a leader who is ready for any change.

Essay Prompt: *What do you hope to accomplish in your life that will define you as a successful leader? (1,000 character maximum)*

Notes

When I was child, I was diagnosed with Acute Lymphoblastic Leukemia and had to undergo major chemotherapy that ruined most of my childhood. Every day I would jump at the chance to be normal because I thought that was all I had to live for. What I found most inspiring at that time was the supportive and caring attitudes of my peers, teachers and family members. Since overcoming that adversity, I have worked to make my goal of curing cancer a reality.

What I truly dream of is a future where my success matters, a future where I don't have to be afraid if my child or any other child has to live through the same maliciousness that cancer provides.

Not only will I accomplish my lifelong goal of preventing cancer, but I will create an internship for high school students within the healthcare profession as well. By accomplishing the goals that I set out for myself, I hope to be acknowledged by the community, my friends and more importantly, my family as a leader that they can look up to.

> Say "I will" instead of "I want to." This shows your determination.

Essay Prompt: *Name one person (other than a family member) who has influenced your life or who inspires you and how. (1,000 character maximum)*

"Can you write me a recommendation for this scholarship?" I said to her with a hint of confidence. "Sure, just send me the information and your activities chart," she said in a relaxed tone. I have had this same conversation numerous times throughout my senior year. Each and every time, she never turns me down. I always find myself asking, "Why?"

My teacher's name is Keri Hughes and she is the coordinator of the Advancement Via Individual Determination program at our school. I have been in this class for two years and for those years I have been pushed to my limit. Ms. Hughes holds me to a standard of never turning in late work and I have certainly learned that late work really affects my grade.

Every day she encourages me to keep working hard, despite the numerous times that I have thought about giving up. She is the reason that I meticulously write essays day in and day out. Her dedication to expect nothing less than the best from her students makes me a scholar.

Essay Prompt: *Why do you think you should be chosen to be a Bank of America Student Leader and what do you hope to personally gain if chosen? (2,000 character maximum)*

When I get asked about why I should be chosen to receive something, I find that those questions are always the hardest to answer. *I have always tried to be the kind of person who does not brag about my own deeds or the things that I have accomplished, but, as I progressively become older, I realize that those questions are becoming more common and I must answer them.*

Being a high school senior is hectic and tiresome work. Whoever said it was the best year of high school must have been pulling my leg. I can honestly say that senior year is no time to slack off or develop Senioritis by any means. *Sometimes being a leader means showing the audacity to spend one more hour than your friend finishing college applications or scholarships. Being a leader means having the initiative to do something for you. It means believing in your ability to compete with students around the nation, regardless of whether you know where they are coming from.* I think that because of my ability to be confident in my own work ethic and credentials, I should be chosen as a Bank of America Student Leader. I exemplify leadership by tutoring my peers and going out to the community to give presentations. I also show that I can commit my full time and effort to this program.

Like any person who wants to succeed, I want to be known for accomplishing something. Every time I think about getting involved with something new, I ask myself, "How is this going to make me more well-rounded?" *To be honest, I want to develop a new sense of how others I don't know react to things. I want to meet, listen and understand where everyone is coming from and their struggles to get where they want to go.* Being a Student Leader will provide me with a network that can keep me connected with various students like me who may or may not like to talk about themselves all the time.

Every person is a leader in a different way. Perhaps we will be able to create friendships because of that.

 Do you think this essay is successful? Why?
- "What makes this essay successful is the way it starts each paragraph with a good topic sentence that keeps the reader engaged. The applicant also lists a good amount of activities and shows the motivation he has to cure cancer."
- "When reading the scholarship essay, it was obvious this student was very passionate with his writing. He has multiple ways of guiding the reader to wherever he wants them to go. He keeps the reader's attention throughout the essay."

 What did you learn from this essay that will help you with your own scholarship application?
- "What I can take from this essay is the motivation to make great starting paragraph sentences to keep my reader engaged."
- "This line stood out to me because instead of saying 'I want to,' the person wrote 'I will,' which shows that he is determined to achieve his goal. It makes the statement much stronger and shows his determination."
- "One thing I really liked about this essay is that for the different prompts the person used different types of writing style. For example, in the fourth prompt, they use dialogue that makes the story more advanced, because instead of saying 'this happened,' it is showing 'what' happened."

Theodore Roosevelt Women's Scholarship

Jocelyn Loyd
Portland State University
Jocelyn is going to major in Japanese and English Literature with minors in Spanish and Writing. After she receives her Masters in Education, she will travel abroad to teach English as a foreign language.

Essay Prompt: *Write a 1-2 page essay in which you share with us your career aspirations and explain how this scholarship will support these goals.*

In the den of a brick house on the side of a Georgia highway going nowhere, two six year olds played school in the flickering light. The summer of 2000 was promising and full of adventure as the chubbiest of the pair uncovered a stack of dusty, yellow paged algebra books. Declaring herself as the teacher, she timidly grasped one in her little hands as she brought it back like Captain Black Beard's treasure to the green pop-up table. Her cousin was leaning like a Raggedy Ann doll in a chair as she giggled and waited for the pretend class to start. They could barely read, let alone solve equations, but that didn't tarnish their giddiness. They flipped through the pages, gazed at the 30-year-old illustrations and assigned homework that neither would ever get around to doing, but it was still a great deal of fun.

I've always been fascinated with how to improve education and make it equal and relevant to all students. I don't want to be a policy maker for education; I want to be in the classroom doing the actual labor with the students. **Working in a classroom is the ideal way for me to give back to my community.** There are so many jokes where a teacher's salary is the punch line, and I can tell by my teachers' faces that it isn't always easy to stand before a mass of chatty, rambunctious teenagers. It's noteworthy how they are able to snatch up attention, amaze and dazzle and inspire through their quirky ways of

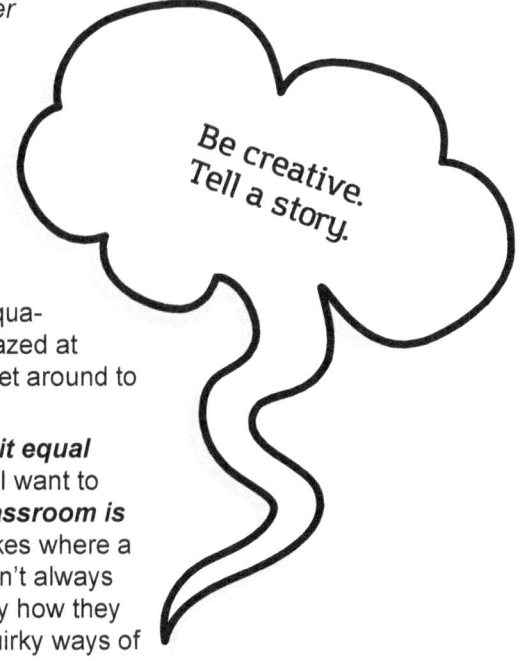
Be creative. Tell a story.

Notes

developing the curriculum. My genetics teacher Mr. Fain is very zany and always has subject-related jokes that are corny gut-busters, Mr. Boyer keeps AP English class engaging by telling us hilarious stories from his unorthodox childhood, and Ms. Lane creates a fun, safe atmosphere in acting class by being approachable and relaxed. The most memorable teachers are the ones who never put on airs; they always take an interest in students and never set low expectations. Most of my success is from the support they've given me. I know that they all believe in me as a writer, as a student and as a future member of the world community.

In eighth grade when I told people that I was going to attend Roosevelt they looked at me strange as if I was joking or had been ill informed about the Rough Riders. *Now I am able to tell them how much I have developed since then and that through this diverse school I have meet positive peers, responsible role models, invigorating inspiration and life-long lessons.* The Rough Riders have taught me to jump hurdles and to climb mountains no matter what. The colorful and unforgettable learning experience I've obtained here will be carried onward as I attend Portland State University to pursue a dual teaching license for English literature and Japanese – I am passionate about both subjects and would be thrilled to work for either field, I have many innovative ideas to make these subjects interesting for future students. I love learning world languages because it opens the gap of communication even wider. **This scholarship will help me study Spanish, Japanese and English literature with a Masters in teaching because my goal after college is to teach English as a foreign language abroad in either Spain, Mexico, or Japan for a few years before I settle down where I am needed in the U.S.** College will shape me into the intellectually involved and evolved leader I need to be.

Over the decade I've daydreamed about being an architect, a neurologist, a filmmaker and every now and then, like all American girls, an actress. As the fantasies expanded into possibilities, none compared to the enticing thought of being an educator, whether in a high school or university.

 Do you think this essay is successful? Why?

→ "This essay has focused on the prompt well and includes several examples of things that interest her."

→ "By including specific, engaging classroom activities, the reader sees that the student is serious and thoughtful about her career choice."

→ "By immersing the reader in a real scene, the author draws the reader into the essay. The reader wants to learn more. It has been almost 13 years since then, and now that wannabe schoolteacher is an 18-year-old Roosevelt senior applying for scholarships, planning for college and preparing for graduation."

If you have a plan for your future, say so and be as specific as possible. It shows you are thoughtful and decisive.

OSAC (Office of Student Access and Completion) Scholarships

OSAC manages scholarships from a variety of public and private donors and is one of the largest distributors of scholarship funds for Oregon residents. Applicants must write personal statements in response to three prompts, **each limited to 1,000 characters**. Note that the target is *characters*, not words. Here's how three students answered the same questions.

Required Personal Statement: *Explain your career aspirations and your educational plan to meet these goals. Be specific.*

Linnette: Witnessing both parents being carried away by ambulances week after week, I eventually wound up spending a lot of time in hospitals. Watching the nurses care for my parents doing all they could to ensure they were comfortable relieved my worries about their wellbeing. I really admired the nurses because they took pride in helping others. Spending much time in hospitals helped me want to become a nurse because I want to help the sick by providing security and comfort to worried families. I believe I can give back to my community by becoming a nurse. *Being a nurse involves focus and determination in academic endeavors throughout college. I will accomplish my career goal of becoming a nurse by graduating high school and attending college with a nursing program.*

Sam: Engineers discover new and efficient ways to do tasks. Engineers perform all tasks such as creating cleaner energy sources, building earthquake resistant bridges or generating genetically modified organisms. When I earn my degree, I am going to be an addition to these pioneers. Through the inventions I will create or contribute in creating, I will benefit society's wellbeing and civilization. *My passion for ingenuity and change has influenced my interests in the world of natural science, especially mechanical engineering.* The rewards of inventing the nonexistent and uncovering the unknown have the greatest impact on my career choice. Although it will take much to reach my goals, I am determined to overcome any obstacles. *I plan to attend college as an engineering major, work in my chosen field and then possibly go to graduate school to earn a master's degree or PhD.*

Warren: Four years have passed since I first developed the dream that has kept me striving for a better education. That dream is to prevent cancer. Just recently I've realized that I want to prevent it, two years ago I might have thought the idea was inconceivable. *An aspiration of that level requires hard work and the will to persevere.* After completing high school at the top of my class, moving into a four-year university won't be strenuous. My predetermined major, Biochemistry, will be waiting for me and Pre-Med won't be far off. I want to continue to expand my horizon. *Exposing myself to a world filled with individuals striving for the same aspirations will help me reach my goal of preventing cancer.*

> OSAC essays are very short with very strict limits about how long your essay can be. You need to be concise. Get right to the point.

Required Personal Statement: *Explain how you have helped your family or made your community a better place to live. Provide specific examples.*

Linnette: I hate watching my mom struggle with respiratory problems. She has trouble with doing many simple things like shopping, laundry, trash disposal and cleaning the house. I help my mom with small tasks such as reminding her to take her medicine. That might be a small task, but if she doesn't take her medicine it could be life threatening. I have no problem in helping her because she is my mother and to see her struggle breaks my heart. *By helping my mom I learned that I am dependable, helping and trustworthy.* I do whatever I can to take care of my mom. Even though I have to sacrifice my free time doing activities that normal teenagers do, I dedicate my free time to her because I love her and if the situation were reversed she would do the same for me.

Sam: In my school, I volunteer at the cafeteria serving food to students who attend after school programs. My duties consist of handing out food and cleaning up the kitchen and the cafeteria after the students leave. *Although it might seem like a job, I love volunteering and I think the students appreciate what I do to help.* The coordinators of the after school program also value my work. *I am reliable and well prepared. Once I make a commitment to help, I do not skip any days.* I volunteer for four days a week, 40 minutes a day of my busy senior year schedule. Sometimes it seems like a sacrifice, but it is my passion to help people.

Warren: Growing up as an outsider to American culture has always negatively impacted my parents. Although they speak English fluently, they were not able to fulfill the dreams that they had as high school seniors. That is where I come in. *Continuously being nudged onto the path of a scholar has instilled within me the principles of success. Obtaining a higher education is no longer only for myself, but for my entire family as well.*

Required Personal Statement: *Describe a personal accomplishment and the strengths and skills you used to achieve it.*

Linnette: I opened my email and read the words, "I am pleased to inform you that you have been accepted!!" Tears of joy and relief filled my eyes. *College always seemed like a dream but in that moment college became a reality.* Sitting in my chair staring at the computer screen in complete shock, I couldn't fathom the reality that I got accepted into the college of my dreams. *Not only am I the first person in my family to get accepted in college but also the first person in my senior graduating class as well.* That moment, I realized all the late nights studying, doing homework to pass all my tests truly paid off. This is by far my biggest accomplishment, so now when I'm asked, "What are your plans after high school?" I proudly say, "I'm going to college!

Sam: Scoring great on standardized tests can promise a higher possibility of admittance to excellent colleges. The urge to earn the perfect score can be every student's nightmare. I spent countless hours practicing on previous tests and reviewing hundreds of pages of test material. *I created my own study routine and tried to stick to it.* Yet, from time to time, I was overwhelmed. *With self-discipline and self-organization, I managed to prepare myself for the deadlines. When my scores were not as high as I wanted the first time, I went back to studying and retook the tests. I was able to improve my SAT score by 200 points and my ACT by 2 points.*

Warren: *Chemistry was never my strongest science subject, yet it was one of the few cohorts to which I looked forward to being in since joining the Oregon Young Scholars Program.* As a senior in the program last year, I had the privilege of choosing my own cohort. After joining the chemistry cohort, my task was to create nitrogen gas. Measuring out tiny portions of sodium nitrite and sulfuric acid was troubling. Too much and the reaction would bubble and too little, nothing would happen. In the back of my mind I kept thinking that the reaction would blow up. *After failing at the attempt once and returning to the drawing board, we ran a second trial and finally generated the gas with the right measurements.* Having had some background knowledge about chemistry made it easier, but ultimately, *not giving up on the experiment and being detail oriented made generating nitrogen gas accomplishable.*

Required Personal Statement: *Describe a significant change or experience that has occurred in your life. How did you respond and what did you learn about yourself?*

Linnette: As I was standing in the gym beside my fellow cheerleaders so excited for the basketball game, a phone call changed my life forever. My brother spoke to me in an urgent melancholy voice. He said, "Don't freak out, but Dad just died." *My heart instantly dropped and a cold rush of wind went down my spine. The sound of the fans in the stands and the basketball hitting the gym floor became mute.* All I could hear was my mom in the background on the phone crying. Over the next eight months I focused on school and I eventually accepted the fact that my dad was now in a better place. *Through this heart breaking experience I have learned that I am a strong young woman and that life goes on and so does the memory of those who are gone.*

Sam: *Education is the key to success.* But when language becomes a barrier, you are left to overcome the most basic aspect of it — communication. *Just four short years ago, I immigrated to the United States from Ethiopia with only an introduction to the English alphabet and a few phrases.* Besides being in a whole new culture, the English language was a big barrier. Luckily there was another Ethiopian student in my class who helped me translate and understand my teachers. I worked at learning the language, and it wasn't long before I got the hang of it. Over the first school year, I improved and was quickly making good grades. I still struggled with the SAT and OAKS (Oregon Assessment of Knowledge and Skills) test, which I failed on two occasions before passing it in my sophomore year in high school. *This experience has taught me that if I work hard at something, I can overcome whatever obstacle is in front of me. If I can learn English that quickly, I can learn anything.*

Warren: Without knowing it, my life was ceasing to exist. *I was losing a war that cost me six years of my childhood and many memories that could not be formed because of the extreme to which this war was fought.* It was a war between my immune system and the maliciousness of Leukemia. I had to bear the pain that cancer brought and the suffering, depressed state of my parents. Whether through radiation, bone marrow transplants or chemotherapy, they were always by my side. As a survivor of Leukemia, I have learned what it means to live a fulfilling life. I will work hard to become the doctor that I know I can be and to help prevent the next child from walking down that same nightmare that I had to endure. Although Leukemia destroyed my childhood, it made me realize my purpose in life; that purpose, to cure cancer.

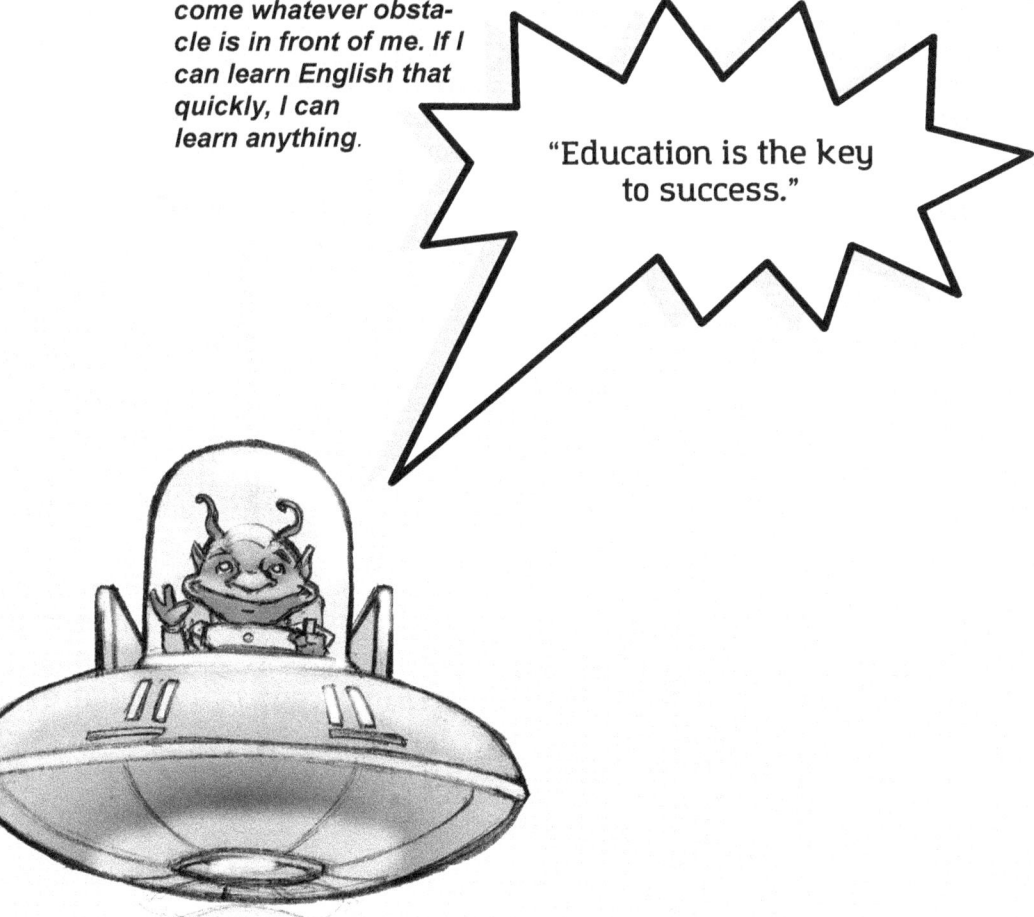

"Education is the key to success."

Do you think these essays are successful? Why?

- "The first paragraph of Linnette's first essay can make anyone emotional because it talks about helping all the worried families. And it gets the reader's' attention quickly."
- "Sam's first essay is good, but he should talk about how it will help other people."
- "Warren's OSAC essays are successful because the author is selling himself. His speech is inspired by his aspirations to cure cancer. He illustrates the importance of never giving up through chemistry. He explains how education is important to help his family. Lastly, what made this essay different from the others were his tragic childhood experiences of battling cancer. Through these experiences the author was able to gain an emotional grasp on the reader, ultimately causing the reader to feel sympathetic, which couldn't hurt when applying for scholarships."
- "Yet, at the same time in his second personal statement, where he explained his ability to help his family through education, it seemed a little weak and he should have talked about how it would help them."
- "In her second essay, I loved the way Linnette said that she can sacrifice her free time for her mother."
- "I liked the metaphor of war that Warren used to describe his cancer, and how he explained it wasn't just an obstacle for him but for his parents as well."

What did you learn from this essay that will help you with your own scholarship application?

- "It is very hard to answer OSAC questions within an essay because they only allow a small amount of words. So, when writing this, you have to know to get right to the point. Warren gets right to the point when answering the prompts. He gives information that's needed and in some cases a little more. Each answer he gives has a new way of drawing the reader in. Even though they were small answers, they still grabbed my attention. I need to learn how to draw in readers so I can keep their interest during my answers. I also need to stick to the subject and avoid drifting off in my details."
- "One thing I can take away from Warren's second essay is the ability to show the reader my aspiration while simultaneously using this aspiration to better the world around me. Also, show some emotion in the essay to make it more compelling."
- "What I can take away from Warren's third essay is that, although I don't have an obstacle as big as his, and cancer hasn't affected me or a close family member, I do have an obstacle that I've overcome. I think if I use some metaphors like Warren did to capture the readers' attention, my obstacle will be explained better and a reader may relate easier. I will also have to make sure to explain my obstacle well in a limited amount of time."

> You don't have to suffer to get a scholarship. Even if you haven't faced great hardship, you are still worthy of a scholarship. Think about *your* life and incorporate its lessons into your essay.

Words of Wisdom

Of course, getting a scholarship depends on you and your ability to "get it done." To spur you on, here are observations and advice from three RHS graduates and three RHS teachers.

Words of Wisdom from Past Seniors

Linnette Meshack: "The scholarship process was challenging, but worth it. My advice to you is don't procrastinate. Be yourself and put your heart into your essays because the truth is, either they're going to like you and give you the scholarship or not, but you're more likely to get it by being exactly who you are and showing that you are dedicated. I believe that if you want something bad enough and you work hard enough, you will get it. So good luck seniors. I wish you all the best!"

Warren Vang: "Scholarships are dreadful. No one wants to sit there for hours and hours just to try to write something that a scholarship committee will read and evaluate. If you're one of the lucky few and receive the scholarship, then everything pays off. However, it's not always like that. I was rejected more than awarded, and sometimes it hurt. My advice for seniors is to always push forward and keep applying because it may be hard. You will want to quit, but it's worth it in the end."

Francis McCollister: "College is a new slate and you will meet a lot of people who are either younger or older than you. Make sure to eat, sleep and study right so you can focus better as a student, because professors will not wait on you. College is way different then high school."

Words of Wisdom from Teachers

Barbara Macon
Barb Macon plays fiddle, gardens and hikes with her family when she's not teaching Health or Computer Applications to Roosevelt students. She believes that going to college and traveling to other countries opened and developed her mind and hopes all her students can have similar experiences.

What is your advice for future scholarship seekers?

Join lots of clubs/sports/activities, go find volunteer work to do, write down what you did and then start early on writing the scholarship essays so you have time to write and refine them. Then ask good writers to take a look at them and give you feedback.

What is your advice for college students who want to save?

I lived at home with my parents during the summer, as much as I really wanted to keep renting an apartment at the university and stay there to hang out with my friends. Meal-wise, I got the cafeteria plan and made sure I got my money's worth out of it. Nothing too fancy.

What kind of scholarships did you get?

I got some money from the state of Illinois (for staying in Illinois to go to college), some from my dad's corporation for being a National Merit Scholar and some from the university in the need-based category. For graduate school, I got some money for the program to be a teacher as long as I committed to teaching four years in public schools. I had to take out loans, but I didn't regret it at all. Having some debt made me get more serious about getting a job instead of just trying to work at a coffee shop, which was somehow more appealing to me. I was forced to stretch my boundaries, and by starting to work through a temp agency, I learned a lot about the variety of jobs out there in banking, manufacturing, construction, marketing, etc.

Jo Strom Lane
Jo Strom Lane teaches Theatre Arts at Roosevelt High School as the Artistic Director for Opening Act Theatre Company. She is also published nationally in theatre education and has conducted theatre workshops for national and state theater organizations.

What is your advice for college-bound Rough Riders who want to obtain as many scholarships as possible?

Attend classes. Do your best. Be involved with a variety of activities. Find your passion. Pursue it without abandon! Then search for every scholarship under the sun, and apply, apply, apply! They can't give you money if you don't go after it.

Did you use any unique or insanely practical tricks to save money for/during college?

No credit cards. Period. If you do get one, get ONE with a LOW balance limit ($100-$250 for example). Only charge if you already have the money in the bank to pay for it. Pay off the balance EVERY MONTH. If you can't control your spending after just one month, cut up the card and wait until you are older with more self-control. Also, I just worked food service so as many meals were covered as possible so I wouldn't have to pay for those. I found a tutoring job so it paid more hourly than the usual work-study jobs. I took more than the maximum credits per semester. Although I had to get tuition waivers for going over the 16 credit cap. I didn't spend money. If I earned it, I saved it, always assuming it was the last money I had, so I had to make it last! Now, even with two degrees, I don't have ANY student loans — all were paid off within two years of finishing school. Why? Because I lived like a ferret even when I had a regular paycheck!

> **Wise words:**
> If you want money for college, you have to ask for it. And that means applying for scholarships!

What kind of scholarships did you receive for higher education?

My high-school journalism scholarship I applied to my Freshman year expenses. It barely paid for books one year, so luckily I was working and got a tuition break from my father working at the community college I attended. I saved all my money working my freshman year to pay for my sophomore year, with some family help. I worked two jobs during my sophomore year, including food service so I could eat. My junior and senior years I received a department scholarship that I couldn't apply for until I was in that department as a declared major. I was so thankful that it paid my tuition, and because of that scholarship, I didn't drop out of school. I was able to work to pay for everything else with my jobs, taking as many classes per semester as I could (up to 21 credits — seriously).

And just for fun, what other advice, anecdotes, jokes, freshman horror stories would you like to pass on?

Enjoy time with friends! Give yourself time to study hard and play safely. It's a time to be on your own, but not go crazy. After all, you have several decades to be on your own!

George Bishop
George Bishop is a social studies teacher at Roosevelt High School. He loves baseball and thinking outside the box when planning his curriculum. He has lots of advice to give to students preparing for college.

What should students do to prepare for applying for scholarships?

Volunteer, do school-related activities, start applying way ahead of deadlines and ask for help from those who know the system.

What is your advice for college students who want to save?

Go on a diet, Top Ramen is your best friend. Just eat simply and prepare your own meals.

What kind of scholarships did you receive?

I had sports-related scholarships.

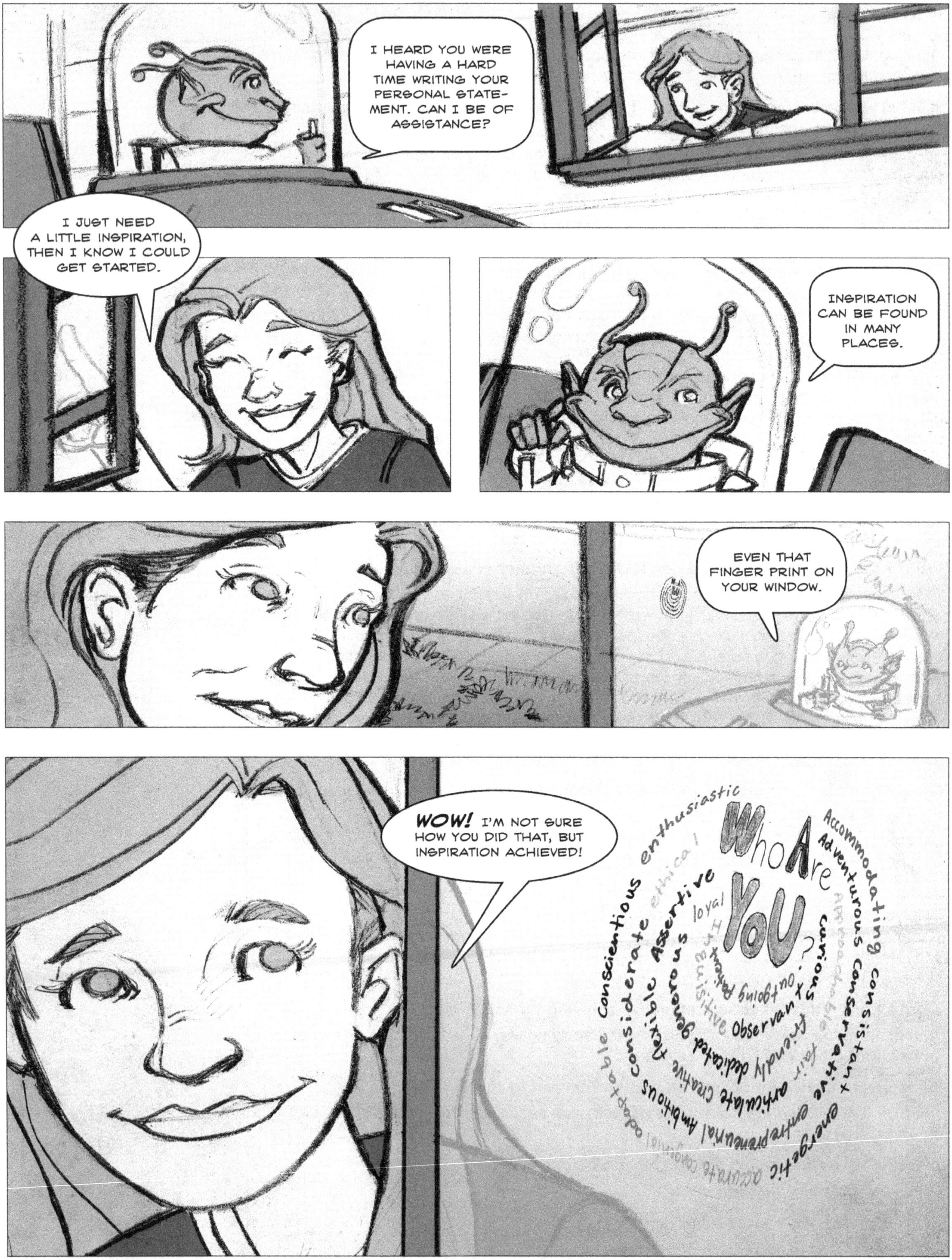

Personal Statements

Notes

The most difficult topic to write about is yourself. For this reason, personal statements can be intimidating. Figuring out how to tell your story (or which story about yourself you wish to tell) requires you to be vulnerable and honest, which can be frustrating. The following activities are designed to help get you started on writing a personal statement.

Describe Yourself

List three characteristics that describe you that you feel are strengths and three characteristics that aren't as strong. Below are some examples of characteristics. Check the ones you think apply to you.

- accommodating
- accurate
- adaptable
- adventurous
- ambitious
- approachable
- articulate
- assertive
- authentic
- autonomous
- calm under pressure
- candid
- cautious
- collaborative
- compassionate
- competitive
- confident
- cooperative
- consistent
- congenial
- conscientious
- conservative
- considerate
- cost-conscious
- creative
- curious
- decisive
- dedicated
- dependable

- detail-oriented
- determined
- diplomatic
- disciplined
- discreet
- driven
- empathetic
- energetic
- enjoys challenges
- enthusiastic
- entrepreneurial
- fair
- fearless
- flexible
- friendly
- generous
- goal-oriented
- hard-working
- helpful
- honest
- independent
- influential
- innovative
- intelligent
- intuitive
- inquisitive
- level-headed
- loyal
- mature

- methodical
- nurturing
- observant
- open-minded
- optimistic
- organized
- outgoing
- passionate
- patient
- perceptive
- persistent
- personable
- positive
- punctual
- questioning
- rational
- realistic
- resilient
- resourceful
- self aware
- socially aware
- scrupulous
- sympathetic
- tenacious
- trailblazing
- trustworthy
- unflappable
- willing
- worldly

Notes

Describe your goals

What goals have these characteristics helped you accomplish? For example: My optimism has helped me to stay positive through difficult family situations.

_____
_____
_____
_____
_____
_____
_____
_____
_____
_____
_____
_____
_____

What's your story?

What story or event is attached to these goals and/or characteristics? What has happened in your life that has contributed to you accomplishing these goals? To what story can you attribute the development of these characteristics to?

_____
_____
_____
_____
_____
_____
_____
_____
_____
_____
_____

Describe your goals
_____

Student Examples

A few students spent time thinking about who they are, what qualities they have and what words or phrases best describe them. How would you describe yourself?

Ciara Johnson (RHS Class of 2015)

As I have given back to my community, the community has continued to give back to me. I am blessed to have been the Roosevelt Rose Festival Princess and the captain of the cheerleading team. The best thing I learned in my Rider home is that no matter what is happening, people believe in me and I have to believe in myself.

The sister.

The protector.

Student body officer.

Captain of the Roosevelt cheerleading team.

Rose Festival Princess.

Ciara Johnson. Survivor.

Jacob Lopez (RHS Class of 2017)

As a student I am always looking for ways to improve. For example, when I was a sophomore I wasn't getting good grades — in fact I was failing four classes. Rather than give up, I realized the only way I could improve was to work better in teams and to accept feedback. After doing that I ended up passing all my classes and acquiring these two valuable skills. I have become student who is continually exploring ways to become a more efficient while maintaining quality.

Anonymous

A tongue swirling in limitless figurative language.

A tongue of passion.

A tongue of authentic emotions.

Self-hatred evolved into self-love.

Shame transformed into pride.

Bilingualism became a foundation of my education.

Spanish is no longer just the language of poor people.

It is the language of love, beauty, creativity and most importantly of who I am.

Erin Dunnington (RHS Class of 2016)

I am collaborative, adaptable and helpful. These skills have developed over time as I overcame challenges and learned new things about myself. My collaborative behavior has allowed me to work successfully in both small and large groups. I am now about to take these skills outside of the classroom, into my personal life as well as the workplace. Being able to assist others and work well with them, and being flexible has gotten me through tough AP courses, and feeling accomplished after an internship working with my peers.

Notes

Scholarship Information

In this section you'll find information about different scholarships that may interest you. Some are national, some are local. Some are college-specific, some are experience-specific. Read them all to see if you want to apply for any of them. **There are many other scholarships that are not listed here.** Just dig around. Many scholarship websites include links to other scholarship resources, which in turn can lead to other scholarships that can lead to even more scholarships, and so on. Take time to explore the options and you're sure to find scholarships that suit you.

Important! The information about these scholarships was correct when it was published, but **things do change. Do not take this information for granted. You must research scholarship requirements and deadlines yourself** by looking at websites or by making a few phone calls. *Make sure you have the information you need to apply.*

> You must research scholarship requirements and deadlines yourself. Take nothing for granted.

State and Local Scholarships

Act Six Portland

Act Six is for students who want to attend either *George Fox University* or *Warner Pacific College*. An initiative of Portland Leadership Foundation, it is Oregon's only full-tuition, full-need community leadership award.

Award Amount: Full tuition

Deadline: End of October

Eligibility: If you can answer "yes" to the following questions:

- Do you love your community and want to use your college education to make a difference as a leader on campus and at home?
- Will you graduate from high school in 2016, or did you graduate previously in 2015 or 2014?
- Do you live in the Portland area and, if selected, could you arrange your own transportation to weekly evening trainings at Warner Pacific?
- Do you want to attend George Fox or Warner Pacific?
- Are you not currently enrolled at a four-year college? (Students at two-year colleges may apply.)

For more information: www.actsix.org

Al Forthan Memorial Scholarship

The Al Forthan Memorial Scholarship is awarded to an Oregon high school senior from a *family affected by alcohol or drug addiction*. ("Affected by addiction" is defined as follows: you were raised by a parent or guardian who experienced addiction or you abused alcohol or drugs and are now pursuing recovery.)

Award Amount: $10,000 over four years

Deadline: Early February

Eligibility:

- Dependent on essay questions and personal statements.
- Volunteer/community service work necessary.

For more information: http://forthanpdx.tumblr.com/scholarship

Beat the Odds Scholarship

The Beat the Odds Scholarship program was started in 2007 to raise awareness about the challenges that prevent too many of Oregon's young people from succeeding and to emphasize the critical role that education plays in helping students meet those challenges. The Beat the Odds Scholarship is a renewable scholarship for students who have overcome adversity to succeed in school.

Amount: $2,500 per year for four years

Deadline: Mid-September

Eligibility:

- GPA 3.0 minimum.
- Oregon public high school student who will graduate during the year of application.
- Has overcome poverty, disability, homelessness, or personal tragedy.
- Has participated in activities that are helpful to others.
- Has been accepted into an accredited 2 or 4-year college program.

You must agree to:

- Share your story at the Beat the Odds award events.
- Participate in all related publicity.
- Create a short, inspirational video about your life and accomplishments.

For more information: http://stand.org/oregon/beat-the-odds/apply

Black United Fund Scholarships

Three scholarships for high school students are offered through the Black United Fund: the ACCESS Scholarship, the Ron Herndon Scholarship and the Inspiring Hope Scholarship.

For more information on these scholarships: http://bufor.org/index.php/site/programs-and-services/black-united-fund-scholarships

Ron Herndon Scholarship

This scholarship is for African-American students graduating from high schools in Oregon and S.W. Washington.

Award Amounts: $1,500-$2,000

Deadline: Mid-January

Eligibility:

- High school student or currently enrolled community college/transfer student.
- GPA of 2.0-3.0 for high school student; 2.5 minimum for transfer student.
- Will attend a four-year university or college.
- Reside in Oregon or SW Washington.
- African/African-American/Black/Afro Descent.
- Demonstrate financial need.

For more information: http://bit.ly/2016BUFScholarships

ACCESS Scholarships

These scholarships are related to specific universities. Each scholarship has its own award amount, student requirements and application instructions. Students must complete and submit the Common Application and/or other appropriate application materials to their selected universities in order to be eligible for these scholarships. Must apply and meet acceptance requirements to receive this scholarship.

Award Amount: Varies. See details below.
Deadline: Mid-January
Eligibility: Varies
For more information: http://bit.ly/2016BUFScholarships

- **Concordia University/Johnson Scholars Scholarship**
  Award Amount: $8,000
  Deadline: Mid-January
  Eligibility: See website for eligibility requirements.
  For more information: www.cu-portland.edu

- **Lewis & Clark College**
  Award Amount: $10,000 to full unmet need
  Deadline: November 1 for Early Action Admission; February 1 for Regular Decision Admission.
  Eligibility: See website for eligibility requirements.
  For more information: www.lclark.edu

- **Pacific University Scholarship**
  Award Amount: $10,500 to full unmet need
  Deadline: March 1
  Eligibility: See website for eligibility requirements.
  For more information: www.pacificu.edu

- **Reed College Scholarship**
  Award Amount: $10,000 to full unmet need
  Deadline: November 15 for Early Decision I; December 20 for Early Decision II; January 15 for Regular Decision
  Eligibility: See website for eligibility requirements.
  For more information: www.reed.edu

- **University of Portland Scholarship**
  Award Amount: $12,000
  Deadline: January 15 for Priority Admission
  Eligibility: See website for eligibility requirements.
  For more information: www.up.edu

- **Willamette University Scholarship**
  Award Amount: $15,000
  Deadline: December 1 for Early Action II Admissions; February 1 for Regular Admissions
  Eligibility: See website for eligibility requirements.
  For more information: www.willamette.edu

Inspiring Hope Scholarship

The Black United Fund and Pathfinders of Oregon have partnered together to offer the "Inspiring Hope: Students Impacted by the Criminal Justice System" Scholarship for the 2015-2016 academic year. This scholarship is for those who are related to a family member that is currently or was formally incarcerated.

Award Amounts: $1,250
Deadline: January

Eligibility:
- GPA of 2.50 or higher.
- Parent and/or family member involved in the criminal justice system.
- Currently enrolled as a high school senior and will be a freshman in college for the 2015-2016 academic school year.
- Applicant must reside in the state of Oregon or SW Washington

For more information: http://bitly/BUFScholarships

César E. Chávez Leadership Conference Scholarship (CECLC)

The CECLC scholarship provides Latino students with the opportunity to further their academic and technical potential as they prepare to become leaders. Scholarships are offered each year for full-time study at an accredited institution of the student's choice.

Award Amount: $1,000

Deadline: Mid-January

Eligibility:
- Latino ancestry or from a seasonal farm worker family.
- Graduating high school senior from a participating School District or Regional ESD.
- Plan to enroll as a student at a two or four year public or private, accredited post-secondary institution in the United States in the fall.

For more information: www.cecleadershipconference.org/college-scholarships/

Dr. Ethel Simon-McWilliams Scholarship

"If you have stumbled academically at some point due to circumstances beyond your control such as health or personal programs, this scholarship is a good match for you."

Award Amount: $2,500 maximum

Deadline: End of March/Beginning of April

Eligibility:
- GPA between 2.5-2.85 (GPA over 2.85 does not qualify).
- 11th grade African American students (U.S. citizen).
- Attend and graduate from a Portland public high school
- Exhibit potential for college/university success.

For more information: http://bufor.org/index.php/site/programs-and-services/dr-ethel-simon-mcwilliams-scholarship

Education First Scholarship

The Education First Scholarship is for high school seniors in low-income communities who attend schools with historically low percentages of college applicants. Successful applicants have overcome adversity and are striving for goals that many of their peers may not share. Education First's aim is to invest in individuals who will positively affect their communities.

Amount: $4,000; $1,000 honorable mention

Deadline: January

Note: To apply, download an application from your high school or ask your counselor.

Eligibility:
- Must attend participating high schools in Seattle, Portland, San Francisco, Los Angeles, Denver or Austin.

Notes

- Submit a written application.

For more information: www.educationfirst.org

Future Connect Scholarship

Future Connect is a partnership between businesses, colleges and communities to help students find success at the next level of college or their career. Every year, close to 20 students receive this scholarship.

Amount: $600 to $3,400

Deadline: The application goes live on the PCC website in the first week of December. Priority will be given to those applicants who complete the application earliest.

Eligibility:

- High school graduate with a diploma or GED.
- Graduate from high schools within Multnomah County, Hillsboro School District and the City of Beaverton.
- Interest in attending one of these schools:
  - Portland Community College (PCC)
    - 200 scholarships awarded each year
  - Mount Hood Community College (MHCC)
    - 30 scholarships awarded each year.
- Participation in Summer Works or Summer Youth Connect Partner programs given priority.

For more information: www.pcc.edu/futureconnect or www.mhcc.edu/futureconnect

---

Hispanic Metropolitan Chamber Scholarship

This renewable scholarship for students of Hispanic ancestry is often matched by many local colleges and universities.

Award Amount: $2,000-$5,500

Deadline: Late January

Eligibility:

- U.S. citizen or legal resident.
- Hispanic ancestry, residing in Oregon or Clark County, Washington.
- GPA of 3.0 or higher.
- Enrolled by September in an accredited community college, four-year college or university.

For more information: www.hmccoregon.com/scholarships/apply/

Kaiser Permanente Health Care Career Scholarship

This scholarship is generally awarded to people who are interested in going into the medical or dental care fields.

Amount: $2,000

Deadline: Mid-December

Eligibility:

- GPA of 2.5 (weighted) or higher.
- High school senior.
- Plan to pursue a career in the medical or dental health care field.
- Reside and attend high school in the Kaiser Permanente Northwest service area at an approved high school.

- Be enrolling at a U.S.-accredited college or university as a full-time, degree- or certificate-seeking first-year student.
- Preference is given to applicants who are fluent in two languages, first generation college students and underrepresented ethnic groups.

For more information: http://share.kaiserpermanente.org/article/northwest-health-care-career-scholarship-program/

Neil Kelly Memorial Scholarship (also known as the Albina Rotary Scholarship)

The Neil Kelly Memorial Scholarship is dedicated to recognizing high school seniors who live in the Albina Rotary service area for their dedication to their communities. Although they all earn good grades, the higher selection criteria for our committee is their passion for community in all its forms: family, school, church and volunteer community organizations.

Award Amount: $2,000

Deadline: Mid-April

Eligibility:
- GPA of 2.75 or higher.
- Live in North/ Northeast Portland.

For more information: www.neilkelly.com/blog/albina-rotary-club-neil-kelly-memorial-scholarship/

OSAC (Office of Student Access and Completion)

OSAC manages more than 475 scholarships from a variety of public and private donors and is one of the largest distributors of scholarship dollars for Oregon residents. Be sure to check its catalogue of scholarships because you may qualify for several scholarships that emphasize talents, artistic skill, athletic interest or career interest. OSAC scholarships may be used only at U.S. institutions eligible to participate in Title IV federal student aid programs (U.S. military academies are not eligible).

Amount: Award amounts range from $500 to $10,000 or more.

Deadline: February 1 (early bird deadline); March 1 (final deadline). Early-bird applicants qualify for an additional $500 scholarship.

Eligibility:
- Be a U.S. citizen, or an eligible noncitizen in the United States for other than a temporary purpose, and intend to become a permanent resident of the United States.
- Be an Oregon resident. Residency is usually established when an independent student or the parents of a dependent student have been in continuous residency in Oregon for 12 months before enrollment.
- For exceptions, such as tribal residency, see the definition of Oregon resident on the OSAC website.
- Be an Oregon graduating high school student during the current academic year, or a GED or home-schooled graduate, or a first-time college freshman, undergraduate, or graduate student.
- Have Oregon listed as your home of record if you are U.S. military personnel.
- Not owe a refund on an educational grant or be in default on any educations loans.

For more information: www.oregonstudentaid.gov/scholarships.aspx

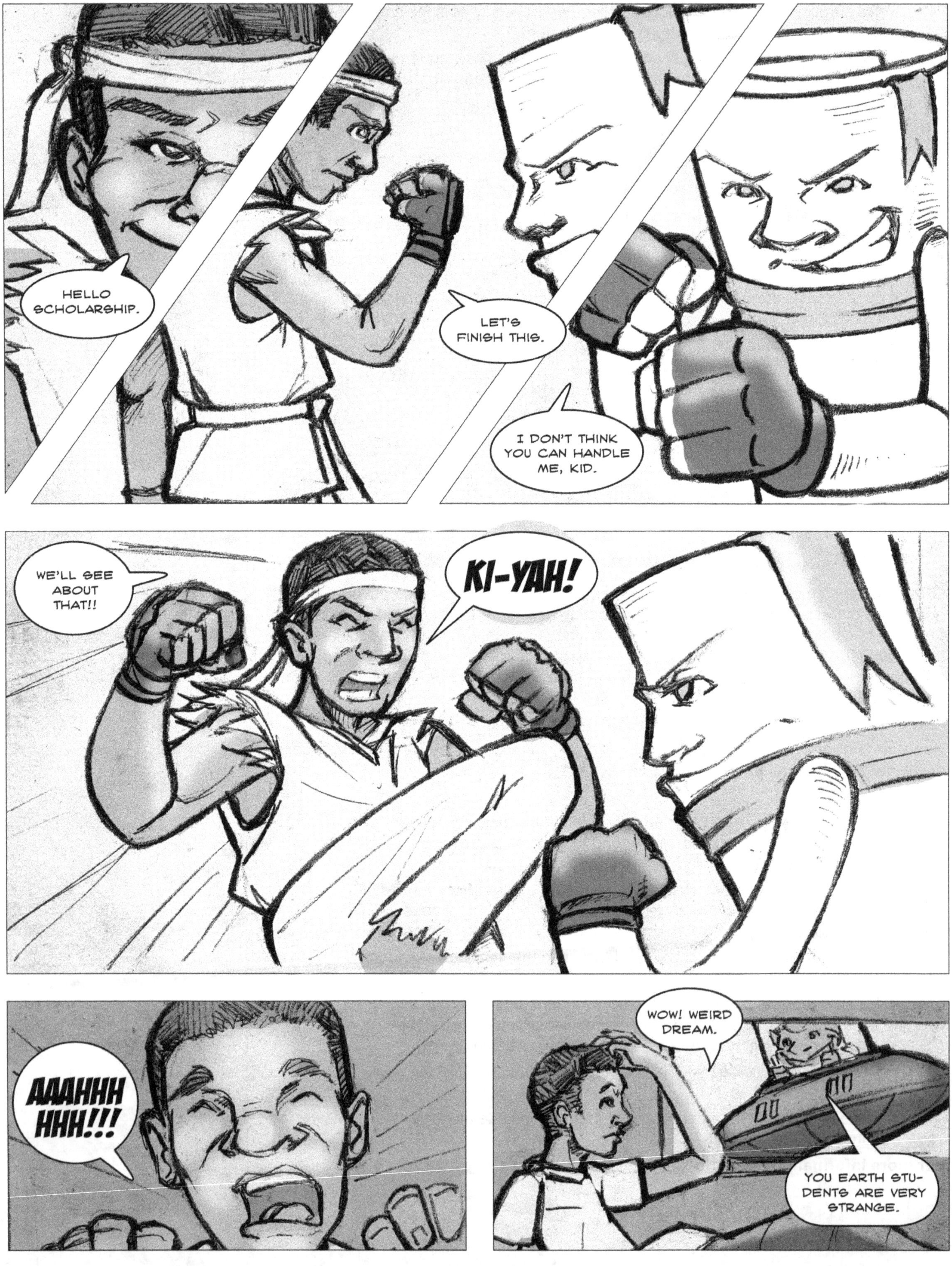

Skanner Foundation Scholarship

The Skanner Scholarship emphasizes active service. Winners are chosen based on their financial, educational and community involvement.

Amount: $500 – $1,000

Deadline: Mid-October

Eligibility:

- Undergraduate student or high school student transitioning to college.
- GPA of 2.5 or higher.
- Attending a post secondary, accredited institution or planning to attend.
- Plans to attend school for entire academic year carrying 12 credit hours per quarter.
- 20 hours of "active" community service within past 12 months with certified documentation.
- Leadership involvement.

For more information: www.theskanner.com/foundation/scholarship

National Scholarships

Dell Scholars Program

"Our GPA requirement is Grit, Potential and Ambition: 'Grit' by overcoming personal challenges in your life related to your family, school or community; 'Potential' by participating in college readiness programs and seeking out academic rigor; 'Ambition' by dreaming of obtaining a college degree."

Award Amount: $20,000, a laptop, textbook credits and ongoing support and assistance.

Deadline: Mid-January

Eligibility:

- GPA of 2.75 or higher.
- Will graduate from accredited high school.
- Has been participating in a Michael & Susan Dell Foundation-approved college readiness program in grades 11 and 12 (e.g. AVID, Gear UP, Upward Bound, ASPIRE).
- Demonstrated need for financial assistance.
- Eligible to receive a Federal Pell Grant in first year of college.
- Planning to enroll full-time in a bachelor's degree program at an accredited higher education institution in the fall directly after your graduation from high school.

For more information: www.dellscholars.org

Gates Millennium Scholarship

This scholarship gives qualifying students an opportunity to complete an undergraduate college education in any discipline area of interest. Continuing Gates Millennium Scholars may request funding for a graduate degree program in one of the following discipline areas: computer science, education, engineering, library science, mathematics, public health or science.

Amount: $500,000. Covers all costs of college — tuition, books and housing — through graduate school, potentially through a PhD. program.

Deadline: Mid-January

Eligibility:

- GPA 3.3 or higher on an unweighted 4.0 scale or have earned a GED.
- African American, American Indian/Alaska Native, Asian & Pacific Islander American or Hispanic American.
- Citizen, national or legal permanent resident of the United States.
- Will enroll for the first time at a U.S.-located, accredited college or university (see website for exceptions).
- Will be full-time, degree-seeking, first-year student.
- Have demonstrated leadership abilities through participation in community service, extracurricular or other activities.
- Meet the Federal Pell Grant eligibility criteria.

For more information: www.gmsp.org/publicweb/aboutus.aspx

National Health Corps Scholarships

Sponsored by U.S. Department of Health and Human Services, this scholarship is for students who plan to work in the field of health services. It can be awarded for as many as four years. If granted this scholarship, you must agree to work in a Health Professional Shortage Area (HPSA) — places around the U.S. and U.S. territories that need health care professionals — in return for each year (or partial year) of support.

Amount: $30,000 - $50,000

Deadline: Late September

Eligibility:

- U.S. citizen or U.S. national
- Full-time student at an accredited school.
- Pursuing a degree in an NHSC-eligible discipline:
    - Medicine (MD or DO)
    - Dentistry (DDS or DMD)
    - Nurse Practitioner
    - Certified Nurse-Midwife
    - Physician Assistant
- Only those students who are committed to practicing primary care and are able to relocate based on the needs of the NHSC in underserved communities should consider becoming a scholar in the NHSC SP.

For more information: http://nhsc.hrsa.gov/scholarships/applicationprocess

QuestBridge National College Match

The QuestBridge National College Match is designed for high school seniors who have shown outstanding academic ability despite facing economic challenges. It allows you to apply early to up to eight partner colleges and rank them in order of preference. QuestBridge then works with those colleges to select the best school for you. The list of partner colleges can be found here: www.questbridge.org/partner-colleges/overview-listing.

Amount: A full, four-year scholarship

Deadline: Late September

Eligibility:

- U.S. Citizens and Permanent Residents currently attending high school in the United States.
- Must graduate from high school during or before the spring or summer.

For more information: www.questbridge.org/for-students/ncm-national-college-match

College-Specific Scholarships

Almost every college offers specialized scholarships based on academic, athletic or artistic achievement during high school. The financial aid pages on the website of the college of your choice will show specific scholarships you may qualify for. Many require that you be registered for the college before you apply. **Be sure to check deadlines for each college.**

Academic Scholarships

Your GPA and standardized test scores can be your ticket to college. Most universities offer renewable merit-based scholarships based on the student's GPA and/or test scores that are included in the university's application for admission. Colleges often title these as *Presidential* or *Honors Scholarships*.

Having a GPA of 3.5 or above may earn you at least $10,000 of annual scholarships for private colleges and universities. Colleges often offer special scholarships for students who combine academics with extraordinary leadership and service.

For example:

- **University of Oregon Stamps Leadership Scholarship**

    The Stamps Leadership Scholarship —the University of Oregon's most prestigious and generous undergraduate scholarship — is awarded competitively to outstanding incoming freshmen from Oregon.

    Amount: UO tuition, room and board for four years of undergraduate study; and up to $12,000 in enrichment funds to be used over four years to help them pursue study abroad, unpaid internships or other experiences. *The total award is approximately $110,000 over four years.*

    Deadline: Late February

    Eligibility:

    - Requires *both*:
        - Minimum 3.85 cumulative high school GPA on a 4.00 scale.
        - Minimum 1240 combined math and critical reading SAT score or 28 ACT composite score.
    - Demonstrated leadership, perseverance, scholarship, service and innovation.

    For more information: https://financialaid.uoregon.edu/stamps_scholarship

Portland Community College

Portland Community College has hundreds of scholarships available through the school itself and the foundations and private organizations that sponsor them. **For more information on all PCC scholarships:** www.pcc.edu/enroll/paying-for-college/scholarships/.

- **PCC Foundation Scholarships**

    The PCC Foundation awards hundreds of scholarships every year. These scholarships are just for PCC students. Community College Foundations offer many scholarships. Because immigration status does not impact admissions into any community college, anyone admitted is eligible to apply for their foundation scholarships.

    For more information: www.pcc.edu/foundation

These are the top five scholarships awarded to PCC students from private organizations:

Notes

Notes

- **OSAC (see State and Local Scholarships, page 51)**
- **Ford Family Foundation Scholars Program**

  This scholarship is awarded to over 20 PCC students every year — and it provides up to 90 percent of your college costs.

  Amount: Up to 90 percent of your unmet financial need

  Deadline: Late February or early March

  Eligibility:
  - Scholars program: for high school seniors and community college students.
  - Opportunity program for single parents.

  For more information: www.tfff.org/node/106

- **U.S. Bank**

  Around 20 students win this scholarship each year. Almost all banks and credit unions have scholarship programs.

  Amount: $1,000

  Deadline: Mid- to late May

  Eligibility:
  - Open to any high school senior or current undergraduate student.

  For more information: http://financialgenius.usbank.com/available-programs/scholarships

- **Rotary Clubs**

  There are many Rotary Clubs in Portland, and each offers its own scholarship. Every year, over 20 PCC students receive Rotary scholarships.

  Amount: $500 to $1,000

  Deadline: Early spring

  For more information: Find your local rotary club to look for scholarship and contact information

  Eligibilty:
  - Some clubs require you be a member, but others don't have a preference.
  - Find your local rotary club and ask about that club's criteria.

  For example: See the Albina Rotary Scholarship (Neil Kelly Memorial Scholarship) under State and Local Scholarships on page 51.

- **Oregon Community Foundation**

  The OCF awards offers many unique scholarship programs. Around 10 PCC students receive this scholarship every year.

  Amount: $500 to $3,000

  Deadline: Late February or early March

  Eligibility:
  - U.S. citizen/eligible noncitizen & Oregon resident.
  - High school senior or first time college student.
  - Not owe refund on education grants or loans.
  - See complete eligibility criteria.

  For more information: www.oregoncf.org/grants-scholarships/scholarships

Mt. Hood Community College

Mt. Hood Community College has general scholarships as well as interest-specific scholarships provided by the Mt. Hood Community College Foundation and by other organizations and businesses. Most other community colleges have similar interest-based scholarships.

These are some of the program-specific scholarships you can apply for at MHCC:

- Automotive Technology
- Business and Computer Technology
- Cosmetology
- Criminal Justice
- Early Childhood Education, History, Education
- Education, Counseling or Psychology
- Fisheries Technology
- Funeral Service
- Hospitality and Tourism
- Industrial Technology
- Integrated Media
- Language and Literature
- Mental Health
- Natural Resources
- Nursing
- Performing and Visual Arts
- Physical Therapy Assistant
- Physics, Engineering or Math
- Transitions/Transciones

For more information on all MHCC scholarships: www.mhcc.edu/Foundation.aspx

Clackamas Community College

Clackamas Community College also lists hundreds of scholarships on its website, both through its own CCC Foundation as well as from outside organizations. Some are specific to students at high schools in other school districts, such as Canby. Read the requirements carefully. Here are two examples of scholarships listed on the CCC website: **For more information:** https://clackamas.academicworks.com/opportunities

- **Oregon Mini Society (OMS) Scholarship (CCC Scholarship)**
  Scholarship for a full time student with at least a 3.0 GPA, majoring in Collision Repair and Refinishing.
  Amount: $2,000
  Deadline: First of September

- **Coca-Cola Scholars Foundation (External Scholarship)**
  Students are recognized for their capacity to lead and serve, and their commitment to making a significant impact on their schools and communities.
  Amount: Up to $20,000
  Deadline: End of October

Other Scholarship Opportunities

Diversity Scholarships

Most colleges offer diversity scholarships that encourage people of color to attend their campus. If you are a person of color and you know which college you plan to attend, be sure to look for that university's diversity scholarship.

Examples:

- **Western Oregon University Diversity Scholarship**

    WOU is committed to recognizing and supporting outstanding students from diverse cultural, educational and economic backgrounds and with unique talents, interests and life experiences.

    Amount: $4,000 per year

    Deadline: Late February

    Eligibility:
    - High school senior or transfer student.
    - Meet freshman admission requirements for WOU.
    - Must be a U.S. Citizen or Permanent Resident.
    - First-generation status (neither parent graduated from college).
    - Show community service, leadership, activities and commitment to social activism.

- **Portland State University Diversity Scholarship**

    The scholarship is a renewable, undergraduate resident tuition-remission, excluding fees. All Diversity Scholars be a U.S. citizen or permanent resident.

    Amount: $6,500

    Deadline: Mid-October

    Eligibility:
    - Oregon resident.
    - Financial need (federally defined).
    - First-generation college student (neither parent has a 4-year college degree from a U.S. university).

Immigration Status Scholarships

Immigration status does not impact admissions into any Oregon community college, so anyone admitted is eligible to apply for their foundation scholarships. Counseling Centers in most high schools have a binder of scholarships available to undocumented students.

Employee-Dependent Scholarships

Many employers offer special scholarships for children of their employees. Be sure to check with your parents' employers to see if they offer scholarships.

Optimist Scholarship

The Optimist Scholarship is primarily for students planning to attend a community college.

Award Amounts: $1,500

Deadline: Information on when and how to apply is available through the counseling office at Roosevelt High School.

Roosevelt-Specific Scholarships

Two scholarships are provided for Roosevelt students. Get application forms from school counselors starting in March.

- **John and Mary Mock Perpetual Memorial Scholarship (for RHS Senior Men)**

    This scholarship can be used at Oregon four-year colleges.

    Award Amounts: $2,000-$10,000

    Eligibility:
    - Roosevelt senior man.
    - GPA of 3.0 or higher.
    - School/community involvement.

- **Theodore Roosevelt Women's Scholarship (for RHS Senior Women)**

    This scholarship can be used at any two- or four-year college.

    Award Amounts: $2,000-$10,000

    Eligibility:
    - Roosevelt senior woman.
    - GPA of 3.0 or higher.
    - School/community involvement.

Notes

Letters of Recommendation

When it comes to applying for scholarships or colleges, the scholarship review teams want to know more about you. Now, I bet you're thinking, "but I wrote a three-page essay for that college about who I am and what I do!" Well, take a chill pill and calm down, because we didn't get to the details yet. Anyway, reviewers want to see you from a different set of eyes. No, not taking their eyes out and switching them with someone else's like in those weird and gory scary movies. Instead, they want to get to know you from someone else's point of view.

That's when the Letter of Recommendation comes to your rescue. A Letter of Recommendation is a letter from someone you've worked with and who can write about you. It shows reviewers what type of person you are from other people's perspectives.

Tips for Getting Good Letters

Sometimes it can be hard to choose who you want to write your letter and also when you should ask. Here are some tips that will help you stop all that head scratching.

- Choose a teacher or supervisor that you've worked with and known for a while, or a teacher who has noticed your improvement in their class.
- Be sure to ask them **two or three weeks before** it is needed. Many of your letter writers are busy and if you tell them when it's close to due date, it would be very difficult for them to give it to you on time.
- Give the person who is writing your letter attributes that you think are good about you, especially those that are related to the specific scholarship.
- It's best to ask for recommendation letters early, like possibly during your junior year or the very beginning of senior year.
- Give **your transcript** to the person who is writing the recommendation letter.
- Give the person who is writing your letter a copy of the **expectations** (length, content, **due date**) and what you think is important about you.
- Give them your activity sheet and current resume and make sure both are updated!
- Provide a **copy of the essay** you are submitting with your application.
- Share the application materials or the link to the **website for the scholarship** with the directions for recommenders or the address for sending the letters.
- If the person who is writing your letter is very busy, consider writing a **draft of the letter** for them so they can refine it based on their experience and submit it before your deadline.
- Family members or close friends cannot write letters of recommendation.

Sample Letters of Recommendation

It helps to give people who are writing your support letters an example so they can see how to write a convincing one.

Sample #1

I am delighted to write this letter of recommendation on behalf of <NAME>. I have known <NAME> since she enrolled at Roosevelt High School as a freshman and have had the pleasure of being her English Language Arts teacher for the past two years.

<NAME> is a consummate problem solver. Faced with a challenging equation or word problem, she leaps to the task with confidence that she can work through the problem and arrive at the correct answer. Along the way, she enjoys the process. <NAME> will be the first to tell you that math is among her favorite subjects and one area in which she outperforms her peers. Getting a late start in high school math due to necessary ESL classes and schedule complications, <NAME> made up for lost time by taking Advanced Algebra and Geometry in her junior year, and this year she is enrolled in Pre-Calculus. Her love for problem solving extends to an avid interest in taking environmental science courses, including Environmental Science in tenth grade and Earth Science and Oceanography in eleventh

grade. She often seeks to understand current environmental issues and delving into possible solutions by doing independent research through the Internet.

Without a doubt, **<NAME>**'s most impressive performance as a student has been in the humanities — especially with languages and literacy. Originally from <PLACE>, **<NAME>** arrived as a newcomer from a United Nations camp in <Place> at age fifteen. She entered Roosevelt High School as a ninth grader with four languages solidly under her belt — <LANGUAGE>, <LANGUAGE>, Swahili and French. However, she did not know one word of English. Nonetheless, all of the instruction in her classes was in English and, because of her amazing facility with languages and determination to succeed, **<NAME>** made meteoric progress in her development of English.

Her transcript, with high grades in English language arts, science, social studies and even Spanish as a junior, reflects **<NAME>**'s skill in learning languages. She even recently told me that she considers one of her greatest personal strengths to be her capacity with languages, noting that she often carries on simultaneous conversations in four different languages with her diverse circle of friends. This capacity will continue to serve **<NAME>** well as she embarks on her college career in electrical engineering, a field that increasingly requires engineers to work in a global context, with colleagues from around the world.

In addition to her pursuit of a highly demanding set of academic goals, **<NAME>** has made the time to play soccer for Roosevelt, volunteer in her neighborhood and serve as translator for her family and neighbors. Additionally, **<NAME>** is a role model to several of the younger, female African students at Roosevelt, who look upon her academic success as a vision for themselves.

<NAME> is the face of the global future: a young woman who loves mathematics, planning to enter the traditionally male-dominated field of engineering, multilingual in five languages, a transnational immigrant and a refugee from a protracted civil war. **<NAME>**'s life experiences alone make her a compelling candidate for the Theodore Roosevelt Women's Scholarship, but the high value that her culture holds for education and **<NAME>**'s indisputable determination to pursue higher education and continue with an advanced degree speaks volumes to the necessity of guaranteeing the opportunity to attend college and seek an advanced degree in engineering. Financial need is the barrier that your scholarship could help strip away in order to insure that **<NAME>** fulfills her academic and professional goals. Please, give **<NAME>**'s application your full consideration.

Sample #2

I am writing on behalf of **<NAME>**. I have known **<NAME>** for three years as a teacher and director of Theatre Arts. Right away, I noticed a young woman with intelligence, drive, and passion, as well as someone capable of taking on the challenge of a variety of leadership opportunities. She has proven her ability to exceed expectations with great appreciation for her experiences. I highly recommend <name> for being selected for any scholarship or admission she seeks.

<NAME> is actively involved in theatre. She is enrolled in two theatre courses her first year in the program: Beginning Acting and Technical Theatre and Design. She has continued her studies by enrolling in Intermediate Acting and Advanced Acting, as well as Theatre Design and Technology. **<NAME>** stands out above the rest in her classes with her work ethic, dedication, and participation. She is one of the student leaders in the tech class.

As a Drama Club member, ultimately she earned over 100 hours of meritorious theatre education service, was inducted into Roosevelt Thespian Troupe #7289 as an official Thespian, became the Thespian Troupe President, and has attended every major Thespian event offered: Camp Thespis, Leadership Summit, Improv Fest, Regionals, and State. She has coordinated multiple fundraisers, social gatherings, and community service events.

For productions, she acted on stage in A Christmas Carol, Taming of the Shrew, Flowers for Algernon, AP Theatre, and Senior Shorts. Also, she was selected as the Stage Manager for Alyse in Wonderland: steampunk style for both casts and tech for Once On This Island, showing her versatility.

She models exemplary behavior and a strong work ethic in class, clubs, rehearsal, and production. I found **<NAME>** to be a natural leader. She consistently encouraged others to participate to the best of their ability. I appreciate her commitment and eagerness to learn. She is simply outstanding and would be very appreciative of any opportunity she deservedly would receive.

<NAME> certainly is eager to extend her studies in theatre arts. I believe she is the exact student who would appreciate both scholarship and college on many levels and be worthy of being selected for such an honor.

After working with **<NAME>**, with confidence I highly recommend her for any scholarship or admission she seeks. I can be reached at the contact information above if you wish to discuss **<NAME>** any further.

Sample #3

<NAME> is a young woman who is clearly on a path to become a role model for the African Immigrant community and any community she lives and participates in. She was a very dedicated student in my Health Education class this fall. In Health, she displayed leadership by simply being a stellar student academically and behaviorally, and then sharing her gifts and love of learning with all the students she interacted with in class. Any time we had work in small groups, I knew her group would be functional -- she does not dominate, but she facilitates and makes sure that the group works cohesively. She works well with students of all races and ages.

Her other leadership growth is visible on her resume: I know that <NAME> has been a participant in several helping or personal growth opportunities. When I saw her resume, I was impressed that she had filled her plate with activities I had not heard of before as being available to kids in our community, so I know she is stretching herself and going outside the normal service projects I see our students doing.

<NAME> is not someone who grabs the limelight, but anything she does, she goes at with the intent to do her best and succeed. She was a student in my Health class last semester, and she didn't just go through the motions of taking notes and doing class activities -- I recall her often making connections and extending the learning by asking me questions that went beyond what we were able to cover. It is clear she doesn't just want a strong transcript -- she actually wants the knowledge!

Despite the struggles of growing up always as an outsider, immigrant and refugee, <NAME> has held on to that central goal of her life: to succeed in education and to earn a higher education degree so that she can make a better life for herself. I began my teaching here at Roosevelt as an ESL teacher, and I see the many rates at which immigrants or refugees learn English. I have seen students who've been in the US for six or seven years still struggling in early intermediate levels, while other students with just the right combination of ambition, intelligence and work ethic achieve native fluency and excellent vocabularies in just four or five years. <name> is one of those students, and she will just shrug off this achievement, saying, "You just have to work hard if it's for your own education." I know that part of her linguistic success is her underlying goal and ambition to use the educational system as her path to personal and family success in this country.

She knows that education is her key, so she sets her goals, and just keeps on working the plan to make herself the best student she can be. She will be an asset to any school or program that she becomes a part of. I give her my strong recommendation.

Sample #4

My most vivid memory of <NAME> is from her 9th grade year when she was selected to attend a spring break trip to visit civil rights sites and Historically Black Colleges/Universities in Alabama and Georgia. One of her peers on the trip was a student from Burundi, still learning to speak English and very shy to participate in the intense conversations that evolved throughout the week. In one particularly emotional conversation amongst the group, a few students laughed at a comment made by the young woman, at which point she got up and left the room crying. Despite not having much of a relationship with her, <NAME> and her older sister, who was also on the trip, left the room immediately to follow the young woman and see how they could support her. They spent the next several hours with her, discussing the way their peers had treated her. They comforted her and eventually encouraged her to re-join the group with their support, courageously speaking up to their peers about their lack of respect in that moment. <NAME> actions and words are thoughtful and considerate. She is respected amongst her peers because she is humble, mild-mannered and on a mission.

Another testament to <NAME> solid nature, is the perseverance and commitment to excellence she demonstrated after her older brother was shot outside her family's apartment during the spring of her 9th grade. Her brother was hospitalized for months following the incident and <NAME> and her two sisters, were deeply traumatized. She sought out mental health support and did her best to recover quickly, but her true drive appeared during the summer following the event. Her grades had dropped significantly due to her attendance, but at the end of the year, she approached her teachers to request missed assignments, eventually working through the entire summer to bring her grades back up to a 3.7 GPA. In her own words, no matter what happens, <NAME> always gets right back up and keeps going.

<NAME> describes a future career in Architecture in which she will impact low-income communities by creating safe, equitable living environments for families. Being timid, <NAME> pushed herself to join Student Government and was nominated Junior Class Treasurer and Senior Class President, an environment in which she describes formerly "nodding yes in agreement" to whatever her peers were discussing, but currently growing in her ability to speak up and lead meetings with no adult presence. She also leads our school's MEChA club, a leadership group for Latino students, coordinating annual events without any adult support.

<NAME> is already a force within her community, and I am confident that she will carry this strength and commitment to any college or university she attends. I enthusiastically recommend her for your consideration.

So, That's It?

Senior is the most stressful year in high school because of applying to colleges, looking for scholarships, and taking multiple classes that are making you want to rip all your hair out!

This guide was created by and for those who need inspiration for their scholarship writing, as well as younger high shool students who want to be prepared for the *Invasion of the Head-Scratchers*.

We hope having this book has helped ease the stress of applying for scholarships.

Wishing you well,

Gameti Kalil and the Unique Ink Team

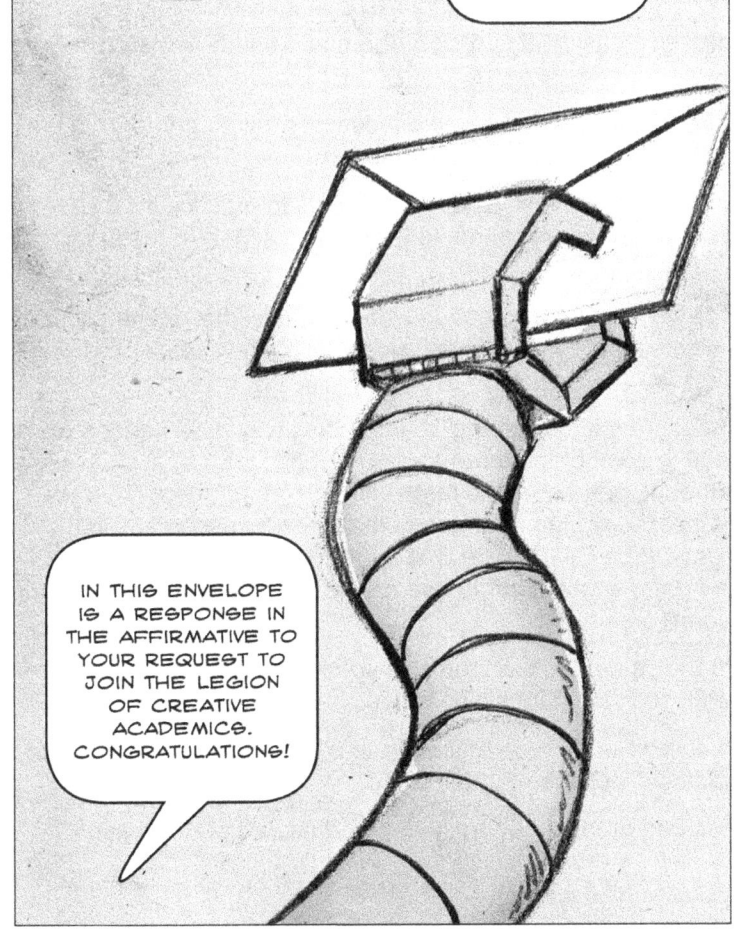

Glossary

ACT: College admission test that measures English, Math, Reading and Science reasoning. Scores range from 1-36, along with a composite score, and 11 sub-scores broken down by subject areas. An optional writing test is offered. Calculators are permitted on the math test but not the science test. Pick up registration forms at school or register online at www.act.org.

Advanced Placement (AP) Tests: Designed for students who have completed college level work in high school, AP tests are given in specific subject areas and are used to determine if a student may gain advanced standing in college.

Admission Test: A standardized test used in the admission process to predict the likelihood of a student's success.

Application: A formal request for admission to a college or university; requires the submission of forms and other materials.

Class Rank: A student's approximate standing in her/his graduating class, based on grade point average (e.g., 72nd in a class of 410; in the "upper fifth" of the class).

Degree: The rank or title given by a college or university to a student who has met certain academic requirements.

Diploma: Certificate issued by a school, college, or university to a student who has met coursework and graduation requirement.

FAFSA (Free Application for Federal Student Aid, www.fafsa.gov): A form required by the government for application to any federal education aid program. A FAFSA is used to determine the specific Federal Student Aid programs that can contribute to a student's total college financial aid package and in what proportions. High school seniors should submit that FAFSA as soon as possible after January 1. The FAFSA is processed free of charge and must be submitted each year a student applies for financial aid.

Grade Point Average (GPA): An indicator of the student's overall scholastic performance.

Grant: A type of financial aid that does not have to be repaid. Generally, grants are for undergraduate students, and the grant amount is based on need, cost of attendance and enrollment status.

Letter of Recommendation: An assessment of the student's aptitudes, abilities and interest, written by a teacher or counselor and used by colleges and universities in the admission process.

Loan: Money you borrow to pay for education-related expenses, such as college tuition, room and board at the university, or textbooks. Must pay back with interest, which can fluctuate.

Major: The subject of study in which the student chooses to specialize; a series of related courses, taken primarily in the junior and senior years of college.

PSAT/NMSQT: Preliminary SAT and National Merit Scholarship Qualifying Test. Enables students to practice for the SAT Reasoning Test and serves as the qualifying test for scholarship competitions conducted by National Merit Scholarship Corporation.

Rolling Admission: The application process whereby a college reviews an application when the individual folder (application form and all supporting data) is completed and communicates the admission decision within a few week of reviewing the folder.

SAT (Reasoning Test): College admission test designed to measure critical reading, math and writing skills needed for academic success in college. SAT scores range from 200 to 800 in each of the three sections (Writing, Math and Critical Reading). By definition, a score of 500 on any section means that 50 percent of the test takers did more poorly than you on that section. To determine your overall SAT score, add together the writing, math and critical reading scores. (That's the number you say when someone asks you, "What did you get on the SAT?") The SAT is frequently preferred, and sometimes required, by colleges on the East and West coasts . Bring a calculator to use for the SAT math section. Pick up registration forms at school or register online at www.collegeboard.com

Scholarship: Financial aid based on merit and paid directly to the student in the form of an outright gift. Some scholarships are given to students who exhibit a particular ability or skill, such as in music or athletics.

Standardized Tests: Tests such as the ACT and SAT provide college admission officers with a comparative standard for evaluating a student's academic aptitude and likelihood of success in college.

Transcript: The official record of high school or college courses and grades, generally required as part of the college application.

Thanks to the community allies who supported the making of this book

Ooligan Press, Portland State University
Per Henningsgaard
Zachary Eggemeyer
Brian Parker
Stephanie Podmore

Dennis Stovall

Interns for Justice, University of Portland
Erika Murphy

Independent Publishing Resource Center
Andrew Farris

Dojo Agency
Jeffrey Selin

Oregon Writers' Colony
Holly Franco
Marlene Howe

SUN School Program, Neighborhood House
Brandon Weaver

SummerWorks Program, Worksystems

The John M. Moreland Fund
at the Oregon Community Foundation

Roosevelt High School
Amy Ambrosio
Keri Hughes
Jennifer Reeves-Eisbach

The Writing and Publishing Center at Roosevelt High School

Where Writing Transforms Our Selves and Our Futures

We believe developing strong, confident writers who proudly express their beliefs and knowledge and who value continuous improvement is central to effectively preparing students for college and life. Modeled on college writing centers, the RHS center will familiarize students with a resource that will also help them succeed in college.

We have designed our Writing and Publishing Center to:
- Enhance academic writing skills for graduation, college and career;
- Raise awareness of young voices and writing in the community; and
- Sustain our near-peer mentoring opportunities and the Writing and Publishing Center itself.

Our Writing Center

A diverse team of well-trained high school and college students provide one-to-one and small-group writing consultations. We hope that our efforts in collaboration with teachers at RHS will enable students to meet the newly required writing proficiencies and to articulate their thoughts as students, workers and citizens.

Learn more abut the Center and its programs at www.rooseveltroughwriters.org.

Unique Ink Publishing

Roosevelt's publishing center enables a team of students to publish professional-quality books that showcase student and community writing and art. In the process, students write business emails, become familiar with Photoshop and InDesign, manage a project using googledocs, create a business plan and write an effective letter of inquiry as well as thank you letters. They also gain an understanding of the emerging world of digital publishing.

Our inaugural publication — *Where the Roses Smell the Best* — is currently sold in bookstores around the community and has been placed in every guest room in Portland's Heathman Hotel.

This fall Unique Ink will publish three additional titles, as well as a variety of children's books.
- *Invasion of the Head-Scratchers: Survivors' Guide to Scholarship Essays;*
- *No Box Can Hold: A Modern Study of Identity and Self-Discovery;*
- *Youth and the Law: A Teen's Guide to Talking and Working with the Police;*
- *The Big Move*, one of several children's books to be published in the fall of 2015.

To learn more about these books check out our publishing web site: www.uniqueink.org

Thank you to these funders for their generous support of the Writing and Publishing Center.

Tim & Mary
BOYLE

Roosevelt's Summer Internship

Invasion of the Head-Scratchers is the third publication of Roosevelt High School's Unique Ink Publishing. Unique Ink is a student-led publishing center whose mission is to work with the community to publish regional pieces. Our diverse writers use the written word to express who they are and what they want to see in the world. The publishing center enables writers young and old to powerfully raise their voices.

Every year students publish at least one book, providing the opportunity for Roosevelt students to:
- Share their writing with the larger community;
- Work with professionals and college students to edit, design, and market the publications;
- Apply their writing skills to all elements of the project communications and management;
- Generate revenue that can be used to sustain the Writing and Publishing Center at Roosevelt High School;
- Research information for publications;
- Be exposed to a work environment; and
- Utilize professional design software.

For more information about the RHS Summer Internship program, **talk to your counselor.**

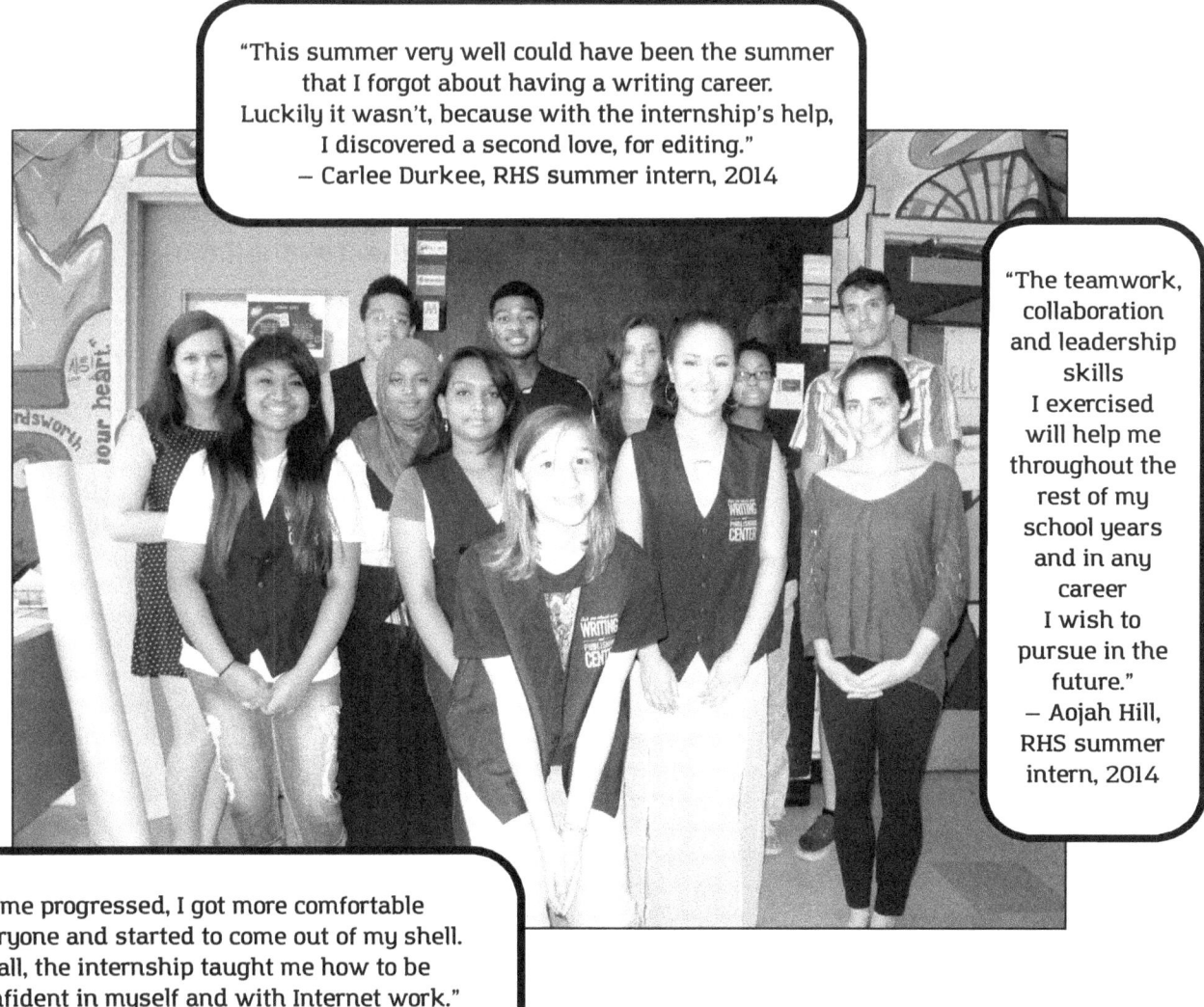

"This summer very well could have been the summer that I forgot about having a writing career. Luckily it wasn't, because with the internship's help, I discovered a second love, for editing."
— Carlee Durkee, RHS summer intern, 2014

"The teamwork, collaboration and leadership skills I exercised will help me throughout the rest of my school years and in any career I wish to pursue in the future."
— Aojah Hill, RHS summer intern, 2014

"As time progressed, I got more comfortable with everyone and started to come out of my shell. All in all, the internship taught me how to be more confident in myself and with Internet work."
— Mariah Radkey, RHS summer intern, 2014

www.rooseveltroughwriters.org/unique-ink-publishing